get a grip on

THE INTERNET

Get a Grip on

THE
INTERNET

JERRY
GLENWRIGHT

CASSELL & CO

First published in the United Kingdom in 2000 by
Cassell & Co.

A CIP catalogue record for this book is available from the
British Library

ISBN 0 304 35593 3

This book was conceived, designed and produced by
The Ivy Press Limited, The Old Candlemakers
West Street, Lewes, East Sussex BN7 2NZ

Editorial Director: Sophie Collins
Art Director: Peter Bridgewater
Managing Editor: Anne Townley
Editor: Peter Leek
Designer: Angela English
Illustrations: Andrew Kulman
Picture Research: Vanessa Fletcher

Originated and printed by Hong Kong Graphic, China

Cassell & Co.
Wellington House
125 Strand
London WC2R 0BB

CONTENTS

INTRODUCTION

THE FOUNT OF ALL KNOWLEDGE

* The Internet is the biggest revolution in human communications since the grunt evolved into the epigram. As important to the way we share information as the evolution of the larynx, it is a revolution that's going on all around us, right now. Dr Johnson said that knowledge is of two kinds: we know a subject ourselves or we know where we can find information about it. For the first time in the history of human endeavour, it is possible to find information about practically any subject, at any time, day or night, from your own home, classroom or office. The place to find it? The Internet.

THE GENIE UNCORKED

information means power

* *Since ancient times, information has been a powerful force*, whether in the hands of politicians or ordinary people. While the great unwashed wandered around wondering where their next meal was coming from, one or two of our more insightful forebears dreamed of societies with free access to information and the power which that would bring – though the notion of accessing the world's knowledge bases from anywhere on the planet using a simple terminal – let alone a hand-held pocket computer – would have been thought of as impossibly exotic science fiction even a decade ago.

'wow - free access to information!'

FOR THE PRICE OF A PHONE CALL

✱ The coming of the computer age radically altered our ability to access information, and the advent of the COMPUTER NETWORK – several computers joined together, so they can communicate and share data – increased that ability exponentially. One network in particular, the INTERNET, a global 'supernetwork', has so changed the way we communicate that our lives will never be quite the same again.

✱ *That supernetwork or 'information superhighway' is a worldwide network of interconnected networks of computers* which offers those who access it a veritable avalanche of knowledge on every topic under the sun, along with the ability to communicate almost instantly with any other person connected to the Internet, anywhere on Earth, usually for the price of a local telephone call.

KEY WORDS

COMPUTER:
a machine that can process data rapidly

INFORMATION SUPERHIGHWAY:
a conceptual global information network, the embodiment of which is the Internet

INTERNET:
a loosely defined, uncensored and largely unregulated network of smaller networks that spans the globe

NETWORK:
two or more computers joined together to enable them to communicate

Different names, same thing

Throughout this book, the words 'computer', 'machine' and 'system' are used interchangeably. So are 'login' and 'logon'.

WHAT IS THE INTERNET?

The Internet is not a network of computers but a network of *networks* of computers, all interconnected or *internetted*.

WWW? NWG?

too many acronyms

A plethora of acronyms

The story of the Internet is the story of technical triumph and a delicate balance of politics, funding and far-sightedness. It's also the story of the most acronyms it's possible to cram into one book. Working groups, committees and research teams all had their part to play, and each had its supremely forgettable acronym.

DEMOCRATIC AND UNIVERSAL

Using a simple computer, a domestic telephone line and a cheap (often free) connection, anyone can access the Internet. What was once the jealously guarded domain of governments and academics is now firmly in the hands of the people.

THE PREHISTORY OF THE INTERNET

* There is a widely accepted story that the US military invented the Internet in an attempt to devise a communications network able to survive nuclear attack. This is a distortion of the facts - but their quest for enhanced information and secure communications did play a part in launching the Internet revolution.

IT'S A REVOLUTION

* Since the dawn of the digital computer, computer scientists have tried hard to wring from their silicon creations every last drop of performance. But it wasn't until scientists began to explore the possibilities for SHARING their limited computing resources that the true performance revolution began.

it's all yours

information is now in the hands of the people

let's
share

OK

scientists   sharing was the key to success

A primary law of computing states that the performance of a computer's hardware will always lag far behind the potential of its software. In other words, it's far easier for programmers to write fantastically complex software than it is for engineers to design the hardware capable of running it effectively.

* *The ancestor of the computer network is the time-shared computer.* To get around the problem of limited access, computer pioneers devised a way of sharing one computer among several users so that each would appear to have exclusive access, thereby maximizing limited resources.

SHARE AND SHARE ALIKE

* With time-sharing, terminals – a screen and keyboard without any on-board processing power – are connected to a remote computer and each is able to maintain a two-way communication with the host via a physical connection. Each terminal is given a tiny slice of the processor's time in turn and, because computers process information relatively quickly, users enjoy the illusion that each has sole access to the computer's facilities. Time-sharing proved to be a great success.

KEY WORDS

HARDWARE:
the physical embodiment of a computer (its circuits, screen, keyboard, and so on)

SOFTWARE:
the programs used to control a computer

TERMINAL:
a monitor and keyboard without on-board processing power, used to access a remote computer

TIME-SHARING:
the division of a computer's processing time among a number of attached terminals so that each user believes he or she has exclusive access

9

I'm sure we could do something more exciting with it

JOIN THE GANG

* The next step on the road to performance was the notion of a network of computers - time-shared machines connected together so that users might access data stored on a remote machine, send messages to one another, and generally interact and exchange information.

scientists realized that computers could be used for communication

KEY WORDS

ARPA
Advanced Research Projects Agency, a US government body responsible for providing funds to private science projects

LOGGING
ON/LOGGING IN:
the process of notifying a host computer of your presence, usually by giving a user name and password

NETWORK:
one or more computers linked together and able to communicate

THE GOOD GET GOING

* The idea of a computer network really got going, however, when computer scientists began to see how users of time-shared systems *spontaneously formed themselves into unofficial communities*, sharing not just the computer's resources but the experience of logging into and using it.

* A significant shift in the way the machines were perceived came about. Whereas previously computers were thought of only as arithmetic engines useful for solving complex mathematical and engineering problems, now computer scientists, psychologists and other pundits began to realize that the machines could be used as a medium for communication.

REDS UNDER THE BED

✱ In 1957 the Soviet Union, perceived by Americans as an all-powerful and aggressive Communist force forever threatening to overrun the 'free' world, successfully launched the earth's first man-made satellite, Sputnik. The shock waves in the West were terrific – especially in the United States, where PARANOIA about the 'Communist threat' was running high.

✱ The launch prompted US President Eisenhower to instruct the Department of Defense to establish a number of new federal agencies, including what later became NASA and – importantly for the story of the Internet – the *Advanced Research Projects Agency* (ARPA).

✱ The aim of these organizations was to seek out and fund the best in private research by US corporations and academic establishments working at the frontiers of science.

✱ The late 1950s proved to be a golden era for research in America's academic and R&D communities, with military dollars flowing freely. At the Massachusetts Institute of Technology (MIT) new labs such as the heavily computer-oriented Lincoln Laboratory were built, whole new departments were created, and many hundreds of fresh, young undergraduates enrolled on a variety of technical science courses – including a new discipline, COMPUTER SCIENCE.

Commercial interests

After graduation, many students from MIT went on to start small specialist companies. In a relatively short space of time, high-tech enterprises sprang up all around the MIT campus in Cambridge, Massachusetts. One such enterprise, BBN (Bolt, Beranek and Newman), founded by three graduate acoustic engineers from MIT, was to play a significant role in the development of the ARPAnet, the forerunner of today's Internet. The company employed many MIT and Harvard graduates, earning itself the title of 'the third university in Cambridge'.

watch out for fur hats

THE FIRST WAN

* The nagging fear of attack from the Eastern bloc prompted several researchers at the RAND Corporation, a defence-oriented think-tank sponsored by the government, to work on the problem of protecting these lines of communication if a nuclear attack should take place.

I'm sure this could work

using public telephone lines was slow and expensive

PAST TENSE

* ARPA-sponsored researcher **Lawrence (Larry) Roberts**, working at MIT's Lincoln Lab, had already extended the frontiers of computer networking by connecting MIT's home-brew TX-2 mainframe to the System Development Corporation's Q-32 mainframe in Santa Monica, California, using a slow connection over telephone lines. *The world's first wide-area network (WAN)*, it established the feasibility of networking dissimilar computers over long distances.

* Previously, few attempts had been made to network computers. Those who made the attempt hard-wired compatible mainframes from the same manufacturer and ran the same operating system over short distances, using relay circuits and cables. It was cumbersome, delicate and slow.

* An alternative was to connect machines

over public telephone lines, though this method was also inefficient and very expensive. Typically the computers communicated by sending bursts of information, and the line between them sat idle while the receiving computer processed the information. *Then, as now, long-distance telephone calls were expensive*. There had to be a way to squeeze more information into a connection and at the same time ensure the fidelity of the messages passing along the network.

NODE NOTIONS

✱ RAND scientist **Paul Baran** began to theorize on the possibility of a *decentralized network of computers*, referred to as <u>NODES</u>, each with the ability to pass on a message to another node using the best route available, with the nodes themselves deciding the best route. If a node was destroyed it would be possible to re-route messages around the network via other nodes, thus ensuring they would eventually reach their destination.

✱ Baran realized, however, that the only way to achieve this would be to *break each message up into blocks and send or switch each one independently* of its fellows. If a node was knocked out, only one block would be lost and at least part of the message would get through. The receiving computer would be able to detect a missing block and request its retransmission.

Americans feared the snip

Block 'n' roll

Baran's block-switched computer network attracted the attention of the military, and in 1965 the US Air Force provided him with funding for further research. He set to work – but when Air Force chiefs insisted on running the project, as well as funding it, Baran bowed out.

13

PARALLEL LINES

* Similar experiments in block switching were going on in parallel with Paul Baran's work, both in the US and elsewhere. At MIT, postgraduate student Leonard Kleinrock had already published the first paper on block switching, as his PhD thesis, in 1961. And in Britain, scientists at the National Physical Laboratory (NPL) were experimenting with similar networking techniques, which they called 'packet switching'

dot dot dash

are you
receiving me?

KEY WORDS

BANDWIDTH:
The space available for data transmission

LAN:
Local-Area Network, a network of computers all sited in the same office or building

PACKET SWITCHING:
networking technique, similar to block switching, devised by Donald Davies

NPL NETWORK

* In 1965 NPL scientist **Donald Davies** – who had worked alongside the famous mathematician and computer pioneer **Alan Turing**, helping to build one of the world's first stored-program digital computers, the Pilot ACE – proposed a national packet-switched network for the UK. But the British government's funding for computer research was vastly different

the future lay in packet switching

but could it work world wide?

the first networks were local-area networks

WHAT IS PACKET SWITCHING?

Packet switching is a way of breaking up messages sent by computers into standard-sized pieces. A large undivided message can tie up a network's entire bandwidth (the 'space' available for communicating), whereas packets from many messages can be interleaved within the same bandwidth and reconstructed by the receiving computer(s), which increases efficiency by a substantial margin. Packets also maximize the fidelity of the messages. If a message is lost or corrupted, it has to be retransmitted; if a packet is corrupted, most of the message still gets through.

from that enjoyed by scientists in the United States. *The ARPAnet project swallowed around $20 million* (though even that was small change by defence-contractor standards), whereas Davies' research attracted finance of a paltry £120,000.

✱ The following year Davies travelled to the United States to attend a computer conference at MIT, where he was able to discuss the new NETWORKING THEORIES. He returned with fresh ideas for building his own network, and in exchange left a present for his American colleagues: the term 'PACKET SWITCHING'.

✱ *Davies succeeded in creating a prototype packet-switched network, called the Mark I.* However, it was restricted to the computers within NPL – what would today be called a 'LOCAL-AREA NETWORK' (LAN). He eventually improved the speed of the Mark I, and went on to build the Mark II network in 1973. Amazingly, Mark II survived until 1986.

it's not the whole story

the message is sent in parts

15

A NEW JERUSALEM

* In 1960 psychoacoustrician JCR Licklider - 'Lick' to his friends and colleagues - published a landmark article entitled 'Man-Computer Symbiosis' in which he described a vision of the way humans and computers should and would, over time, interact. The essence of this interaction would be the computer's ability to free users from excessive toil, enabling them to think and create without restriction. Moreover, computers would make possible vastly enhanced global communications, allowing people to share ideas and information easily.

A MILLION DOLLARS IN 20 MINUTES

Robert Taylor wandered into the office of Charles Herzfeld, his boss at the Pentagon, and pitched to him his off-the-cuff notion of building a network. He emerged just 20 minutes later, having persuaded Herzfeld to fund the project to the tune of a million dollars.

freedom from this excessive toil would be great

computers would do all the hard work

a fast buck

GALACTIC REVOLUTION

* By 1962, Licklider had developed his vision to the point at which he produced a series of memos describing a *'galactic network' of interconnected computers that would revolutionize communications*. Those wired into the matrix, he reasoned, would be able to work as a single integrated unit.

it would be a galactic network

* Licklider's Brave New World ideas caught the attention of ARPA director **Jack Ruina**, who offered him the chance to head the agency's new behavioural-science division. Soon after Lick arrived there, his love affair with the computer led to ARPA founding a new section within the agency, known as the INFORMATION PROCESSING TECHNIQUES OFFICE (IPTO). Ruina sensed that his unique blend of psychological expertise and intense interest in human–computer interaction might lead to important discoveries.

Licklider had a vision

* Licklider immediately set about funding projects that might transform his dream of a galactic network into reality. In 1963 IPTO offered funding to **Doug Englebart**, an electrical engineer who, after working at NASA's Ames Laboratory for three years, had taken a research post at the Stanford Research Institute (SRI), devising new ways to manipulate computers. *Englebart's amazing inventions there included the mouse and the windowed graphics display*, and his work attracted much attention. He, in his turn, was able to find cash for **Robert Taylor**, a young scientist doing research work at NASA.

A STITCH IN TIME

* Soon after, Taylor himself came to the notice of ARPA, where the new director of IPTO, **Ivan Sutherland**, offered him a job. Less than a year later he took over from Sutherland as director. A cornerstone in the building of the Internet was about to be laid.

Bob Taylor's tiresome terminals

The story goes that in a room next to Taylor's office there were a number of terminals connected to the central computers of ARPA's contractors around the US. Taylor soon got tired of moving from terminal to terminal and wrestling with different log-in procedures and command sequences each time he wanted to access one of these computers. What was needed, he reasoned, was somehow to network them together so that it would be possible to access any one of them from a single terminal – racy stuff for 1966.

17

INVOLVING INDUSTRY

* One of ARPA's key strategies was always to rely on private contractors in industry to solve its problems. Taylor drew up a document known as a Request For Proposals entitled 'Cooperative Networking of Time-shared Computers', which sketched out the network project and its objective. However, the nature of the problem meant that the proposal was somewhat vague, and Taylor realized that he needed help in describing just what it was he wanted potential contractors to do.

ENTER THE EXPERTS

* He sought out *network expert Larry Roberts* – the Lincoln Lab scientist who had worked on the TX-2/Q-32 WAN and who had just completed the first transatlantic computer link – and tried to hire him. Roberts firmly declined.

* As director of IPTO, however, *Taylor was a powerful force in Lincoln Lab's fortunes* (the office directly funded more than half its research), and it wasn't long before the Lincoln's boss suggested to Roberts that a move to IPTO might be a good idea.

CONFERENCE TIME

* So Larry Roberts began work on the REQUEST FOR PROPOSALS, and in spring 1967 he introduced his proposals for the network during a special meeting at ARPA's annual conference of research contractors.

KEY WORDS

HOST:
a mainframe computer with a network attached to it

IMP:
Interface Message Processor, a minicomputer that provides a gateway for other computers to join a network

MINICOMPUTER:
a cut-down mainframe with less memory and less storage capacity, requiring only half a room or a room to house it

PROTOCOL:
an agreed method by which a task is achieved

small computer

WOW! it's so small

a minicomputer might only need half a room

PDP-1

The world's first minicomputer was invented in 1961 by the Digital Equipment Corporation. It was called the PDP-1. This machine had a tiny footprint – just 10 metres, in contrast to the hundreds of metres of a typical mainframe – and cost a mere $120,000.

LITTLE BEAUTIES

Computer companies devised minicomputers as smaller, cheaper alternatives to the behemoths known as mainframes. Minis typically have cut-down processing power and smaller memories, but their power derives from their convenience and price tags – a tiny fraction of the cost of a mainframe.

in computer terms small is beautiful

✱ *It was soon decided that the network should be based on the new principle of packet switching*; and that it should have error control, routing and user identification conventions common to every machine on the network, rather than a proprietary protocol for each computer.

✱ These objectives would be achieved by creating a SUBNETWORK of dedicated minicomputers, all of the same type, each of which would provide a 'GATEWAY' to the network attached to the host computer.

✱ *The gateway minicomputers would be called Interface Message Processors or IMPs*, and would be connected using telephone lines. With the IMPs connected into a reliable subnetwork using a common COMMUNICATIONS PROTOCOL, the only remaining problem would be to write a software interface between IMPs and hosts.

19

NETWORK CHRISTENING

✱ The new network was now known as the ARPA Network, or ARPAnet for short. At the end of 1967 IPTO commissioned the Stanford Research Institute to write a preliminary report specifying the network; and by December of that year SRI's Elmer Shapiro, along with several others, produced the document 'A Study of Computer Network Parameters'.

QUEUE GARDENERS

Computer scientists use the complex equations of queueing theory to predict and monitor (among other things) the throughput of data packets in a computer network. This enables them to determine potential bottlenecks and to decide upon the most efficient size for the data packets.

IN TRIPLICATE!

✱ Using this report, Larry Roberts and another ARPA scientist, **Barry Wessler**, wrote a final specification for the IMPs; and this, along with a plan for the network project entitled 'Resource-sharing Computer Networks', was approved by the ARPA's director on 21 June 1968. These guys didn't even breathe without writing at least a dozen reports in triplicate first!

✱ The plan detailed the objectives of the ARPAnet project, and stated its benefits to the military and ARPA's community of researchers. The plan was refined into a detailed series of specifications; and these, along with a Request For Quotations, were sent out to 140 potential contractors in industry, inviting them to bid. By the end of the summer ARPA had received twelve bids, including one from BBN.

going

going

GONE

'what am I bid for this network?'

I don't think much of this queueing theory

nor do I

'why are we waiting?'

HEART'S EASE

* *Larry Roberts examined the twelve bids in detail, eventually selecting the team at BBN*, headed by **Frank Heart**, for the contract. The company had spent more than $100,000 producing its bid, and its success in winning the contract earned it a congratulatory telegram from Massachusetts Senator Edward Kennedy.

CENTRES OF EXCELLENCE

* Meanwhile, several research centres were chosen to be the first connected to the new network once it was up and running. Leonard Kleinrock – by now Professor Kleinrock, at the University of California at Los Angeles (UCLA), and noted for his work in QUEUEING THEORY – was selected to head a team that would provide accurate measurement of the performance of the ARPAnet. *UCLA became the Network Measurement Centre*.

Service centres

Other sites selected to provide unique services for the fledgling network were SRI, where the Network Information Centre was managed by Doug Englebart; the University of California at Santa Barbara (UCSB), then at the forefront of 3-D computer graphics research; and the University of Utah, where IPTO's second director, Ivan Sutherland, was researching interactive computer graphics.

KEY WORDS

GRAPHICS:
a computer's ability to display and manipulate images (as opposed to displaying simple text)

READY, STEADY, GO!

GO!

* To start the ball rolling, SRI scientist Elmer Shapiro was asked by ARPA to 'make something happen'. In the summer of 1968 Shapiro called a meeting of programmers from the four chosen host sites and formed them into the Network Working Group (NWG). This was responsible for deciding how to implement a common network protocol and how the host mainframes at each site would be taught to communicate with its IMP. A difficult task, because at that time no IMP existed and the practicalities of packet switching were almost entirely unknown.

the race was on

A MATTER OF PROTOCOL

* Present at this initial meeting were postgraduate students **Stephen Crocker** from UCLA, **Steve Carr** from the University of Utah, **Ron Stoughton** from UCSB and **Jeff Rulifson** from SRI. From the outset, Crocker and the others realized that the network needed 'general transport services at the bottom with application-specific protocols on top'. In other words, a COMMON PROTOCOL for the actual communications over the network, with separate protocols for any applications that might be devised to run on it.

ok, one over there

the network needed a transport protocol

NO HOLDS BARRED

✱ By the end of the first meeting the group had mapped out what it called DEL (Decode-Encode Language) and NIL (Network Interchange Language). These languages would provide the basis of a protocol for transporting messages to and fro on the network.

'celebrate good times...'

✱ The NWG also agreed to hold regular exchange meetings at each other's sites – the only rules for which would be that there were no rules, that nothing was official, and that anyone could say anything they considered pertinent to the project.

✱ Several such meetings followed, and it was decided that each should be informally minuted. Steve Crocker began to produce notes entitled REQUEST FOR COMMENTS (RFCs), which he felt would be less likely to offend those the NWG perceived to be in charge of the ARPAnet project.

Ringing in the new

Work on the first IMP began at BBN on the first day of the new year, 1969. Headed by Frank Heart, the team included programmers David Walden and Bill Crowther, debugger Bernie Coswell and hardware specialist Severo Ornstein, a one-time geologist who'd been bitten by the computer bug. Another team member, Bob Kahn, had the task of designing a suitable specification for connecting host mainframes to IMPs. The team chose the Honeywell DDP-516 minicomputer as the machine to transform into an IMP. Built to military specifications with a reinforced steel body, the Honeywell was one of the most powerful minis then available and boasted a memory of 24K (12,000 16-bit words) – enormous by the standards of the time, though tiny compared with the computers that exist today.

23

LANGUAGE BARRIER

✱ Given the limited memory of the IMP, the programmers chose to write in assembly language to ensure that the resulting code was both fast and efficient. First though, they had to write an assembler to convert their assembly language instructions into a form the machine could understand.

I'm sorry I don't speak dutch

language barriers can cause problems

001, then 101
1001100110

FAST WORK

computers only speak binary

✱ This they did by writing an ASSEMBLER on BBN's PDP computer and transferring (or 'porting') the compiled program to the Honeywell, using paper tape. At this point, the team had just eight months to modify the DDP-516 and write the Network Control Protocol (NCP) software!

SPEED FREAKS

Before the advent of specialised systems programming languages such as C, assembler was the language of choice for anyone who wanted speed and compact code. Assembly language typically executes many hundreds of times faster than similar programs written in high-level languages such as BASIC and Pascal. The drawback is the comparative difficulty in writing it!

SHIFT WORK

Fundamental to the success and subsequent development of the ARPAnet was the shift in perception that viewed computers as communications devices, rather than as big calculators.

24

✱ The project progressed well, though BBN test engineer **Ben Barker** had to strip and rebuild the IMP several times – wire by wire – to solve hardware problems. Then, just when it looked as if the team couldn't possibly make the deadline of 30 August 1969, IMP-0, the first of its kind, was delivered to the University of California's Los Angeles campus.

✱ Steve Crocker at UCLA was told about its impending delivery just two days before, and stayed up all night to complete the software that would enable him to connect UCLA's Xerox Sigma-7 mainframe to the IMP – *thereby creating the first node on the ARPAnet*.

TESTING TIME

✱ A month later the second IMP was delivered to SRI and connected to the Institute's SDS-940 mainframe using host/IMP software written by Stanford postgraduate students.

✱ *With a connection between the two nodes up and running, it was time to test the fledgling ARPAnet*. UCLA telephoned SRI, and the two teams synchronized the world's first log-on. Intense excitement gripped the teams as UCLA undergraduate **Charlie Klein** asked SRI if they'd received the L he'd just typed at UCLA's terminal. Yes, came the reply. Charlie asked about the O. Sure, said Stanford. And what about the G, asked Charlie? But it was too late, for the world of computer science had witnessed yet another first – the *network had crashed!*

Speaking in tongues

Computers are simple beasts. To program one, you must instruct it using the only language it's able to understand: binary arithmetic (1s and 0s). A computer's hardware circuits operate by being switched on or off, and this bi-state system is most directly represented by binary notation. However, programming a computer using binary is a tedious process and one that is difficult to debug. To make things easier 'high-level' languages such as assembly language and BASIC were developed. The computer can't understand these languages, but an intermediary program known as a compiler translates the high-level language statements into the 1s and 0s the computer can understand.

oh no! It's crashed

GANG OF FOUR

* By the end of 1969 the four sites chosen for the original network were up and running. The third site to receive an IMP, the University of California at Santa Barbara, connected its IMP to an IBM 360/75 running the OS/MTV operating system; and the fourth site, the University of Utah, connected its to a DEC PDP-10 running TENEX.

KEY WORDS

TIP:
Terminal Interface Processor, a kind of cut-down IMP that can be connected directly to a network without the need for a host computer

Error checking

One of the first problems which came to light was that BBN had underestimated the need for error checking between the host mainframes and their IMPs on the subnet. Heart and his team had assumed that the mainframes and IMPs would be no more than 50 feet apart, and that the short connection between the two would rule out the possibility of errors. Consequently, the fifth IMP – the one installed at BBN itself – had to have its line drivers suitably beefed up to ensure the integrity of the system would be good up to 2,000 feet.

always check your answers

ARPANET ONLINE

* Four incompatible machines running four entirely different operating systems were now connected to the subnet of IMPs, and each was able to communicate with its fellows on the network. The ARPAnet was online, and the task of testing it to its limits could begin. The new network performed surprisingly well with only one or two problems coming to light.

RAPID GROWTH

✱ The network grew swiftly during the following two or three years. The first four nodes having been established in 1969, BBN became the fifth a short while later and was soon followed by MIT, the RAND Corporation, the System Development Corporation (SDC), Harvard, the Lincoln Lab, Stanford, the University of Illinois, Case Western Reserve University, Carnegie-Mellon University and NASA's Ames Laboratory.

✱ At first all fifteen used HONEYWELL DDP-516 MINICOMPUTERS configured as IMPs. Then when Honeywell launched the 316, a sibling to its popular minicomputer but costing less than half the price, BBN acquired one and configured it as a new kind of IMP called a TIP or TERMINAL INTERFACE PROCESSOR.

but it was half the price

the incredible shrinking IMP

it's all about subnet configuration

Little IMP

The 316 marked a departure in subnet configuration, as well as in IMP specification. The TIP, a kind of cut-down IMP, is known as a parasite node: it does away with the need for a host and enables terminals to be connected directly to the network. The first sites to use TIPs were NASA's Ames Laboratory and Mitre, a government contractor.

TIP OFF

Built to military specifications, the Honeywell DDP-516 minicomputer featured sturdy construction but at a high price – so when Honeywell launched the 316 at half the price, ARPAnet engineers took to this Terminal Interface Processor like computer scientists to silicon.

ALOHA !

SURFING USA

* Though in its own terms extremely successful, the ARPAnet remained a network alone until Norm Abramson, a professor at the University of Hawaii, built the world's first wireless packet-switched network. Abramson had gone to Hawaii partly to pursue his life-long passion for surfing.

Abramson, the first net surfer

thanks for your packet

ALOHAnet sent data packets via radio

MULTI-ACCESS CHANNELLING

* *Abrahamson got a job as Professor of Engineering, and immediately set about solving the problem of inter-island communications* by devising a radio-based packet-switched network to link the Hawaiian island chain. Dubbed ALOHANET, Abramson's network was funded by IPTO director Larry Roberts.

* Based on the ARPAnet, ALOHAnet uses a simple protocol to get around the limitations of sharing a single radio frequency. Its hosts broadcast packets of data irrespective of what else is happening on the network – though this strategy leads to the possibility of two or more computers transmitting packets at the same time and corrupting each other's data. To obviate the

problem, ALOHAnet receiving computers send <u>ACKNOWLEDGEMENTS</u> only when they get good packets. If a sending computer doesn't get an acknowledgement, it waits a random period of time then retransmits the packet. This protocol is known as <u>MULTI-ACCESS CHANNELLING</u>.

London calling

to me

to you

only complete
packets are
acknowledged

INTERNETTED!

* As well as being the world's first wireless packet-switched network, ALOHAnet became instrumental in a great leap forward in networking. In 1971 Larry Roberts provided Abramson's team with a TIP, which Abramson promptly used to connect ALOHAnet to the ARPAnet. A turning point for the ARPAnet, the *Hawaii TIP was the first wholly separate network to be interconnected – or internetted* – with it.

RADIO WIZARDRY

Today amateur radio operators (hams) using relatively unsophisticated home computers and transceivers regularly tap into packet-switched networks – but in the 1960s the wireless packet network was at the leading edge of technology.

great leap
forward in
networking

READ
ALL
ABOUT
IT!

GOING PUBLIC

* In October 1972 a public demonstration of the ARPAnet was given at the First International Conference on Computer Communications in Washington, DC. Though by now a palpable success, there were still many detractors who remained unconvinced of the future success of packet-switched networks - among them the communications giant AT&T.

amazed gasps

WOW

audiences were amazed

HOTEL SWEET

* *Larry Roberts and BBN's Bob Kahn decided to show the world just what the network was capable of.* They installed 40 terminals and a TIP at the Washington

Triple achievement

A postgraduate student at the time of the 1972 conference, Robert (Bob) Metcalfe went on to great things in the world of computer communications. Hired by Xerox to work at its Palo Alto Research Center, Metcalfe became involved in a project to network Xerox's new desktop-sized computer, named 'Alto'. Heading a team of three, Metcalfe devised a network protocol based on Norm Abramson's multi-access-channel ALOHAnet. The simple protocol would enable computers to transmit data over a single coaxial cable. However, unlike Abramson's ALOHAnet, machines connected to the Ethernet listened to see if a transmission was in progress before proceeding to transmit. If a transmission was detected, the computer would wait for a random period before trying again. Unable to persuade Xerox to launch his invention commercially, Metcalfe decided to market it himself under the name Ethernet and called his new company 3Com – Computer Communications and Compatibility.

Hilton Hotel. **Bob Metcalfe** – later the founder of network giant 3Com and inventor of the Ethernet – wrote a short guide to the conference, explaining how the ARPAnet worked and what it could do.

✱ Delegates from around the world (including Britain's Donald Davies) watched in awe as Metcalfe and others logged into computers at sites all over the United States, ran programs on REMOTE MACHINES, accessed data and downloaded it to the Hilton terminals. Some found it hard to believe that what they were watching was really happening. Others simply couldn't understand it at all.

✱ The event was a great success, until Bob Metcalfe began a demonstration for the men in grey suits from AT&T – at which point the network crashed spectacularly and for the only time during the conference! The AT&T people departed, with their low opinion of packet-switched networks confirmed.

my ass

the AT&T people were not impressed

NAME GAME

Xerox's first two prototype Altos were named 'Michelson' and 'Morley' after the scientists who disproved the theory of an invisible ether filling the universe – so when Metcalfe invented his simple network protocol based on a single coaxial cable, he couldn't resist calling it Ethernet.

I'll call it ethernet

a scientific joke

3Com - Computer, Communications and Compatibility

GROW, MY PRETTIES

* The First International Conference on Computer Communications had been a resounding success, and the network continued to grow. At the beginning of 1973 there were 35 ARPAnet nodes, of which 14 were configured as TIPs, including a satellite link to the TIP at the University of Hawaii; by the end of that year 40 IMPs and TIPs connected 45 hosts to the network, and data throughput had risen from around a million packets a day in 1972 to 2.9 million packets.

the network continued to grow

Secret letters

Working in secret (use of the ARPAnet was strictly controlled), Tomlinson wrote software to handle network email and sent a message to himself by way of a test. His secret application was a secret no more. Almost immediately users began sending email to each other at sites all over the ARPAnet, and it wasn't long before Leonard Kleinrock's UCLA measurement team was describing email as the biggest source of daily packet transmission on the network!

MAIL MAN

* Though primarily intended as a tool for research, a new phenomenon was adding greatly to ARPAnet traffic flow. **Ray Tomlinson**, an engineer at BBN, decided to expand the messaging idea that was already popular on time-shared computers. Users who logged into a time-share system were able to pass ELECTRONIC MAIL or 'email' to each other, and Tomlinson hit upon the notion of enlarging the original idea to enable people to send email out across the network to users at different hosts.

PROTOCOL PRESSURE

✷ ARPAnet testing and development continued apace. In 1973 the first transcontinental connections were made as Britain and Norway linked to the network, increasing the pressure to replace the by now ailing NETWORK CONTROL PROTOCOL (NCP) software with something able to handle the intense traffic and interconnected networks.

✷ BBN's Bob Kahn and **Vinton Cerf**, an assistant professor at Stanford, thought they had the answer. Kahn met Cerf when the latter was working as a young engineer at the Network Measurement Center at UCLA and the pair soon struck up a productive friendship. In 1972 Cerf was elected chairman of a new group, the International Network Working Group (INWG), formed at the First International Conference on Computer Communications.

the perfect
address system

@ HOME

Tomlinson devised a neat solution to the problem of addressing email messages. Email on a time-shared computer had only to be addressed with the name of the recipient, but Tomlinson realized that on a network the host name as well as the user name would have to be specified in order for an email to reach its destination. Musing on the problem, he glanced down at his keyboard and noticed the @ symbol. Unused in proper nouns, the symbol seemed ideal for the job. At a keystroke, Tomlinson had devised the perfect addressing system.

KEY WORDS

EMAIL:
short for 'electronic mail' (messages transmitted over computer networks)

we'll make a packet

SATELLITE SOLUTION

* Bob Kahn briefed Vinton Cerf about a satellite packet network then being developed by BBN, SRI and Collins Radio that would enable a form of mobile networking.

coffee and TCP at Stanford

protocols from space

A DOSE OF TCP

At a series of informal seminars, Cerf described the work on the satellite project to his Stanford seminar students (a group that included Richard Karp and Bob Metcalfe, among others). From these talks came the germ of a new protocol called TRANSPORT CONTROL PROTOCOL, or TCP. The protocol would be able to handle the tremendous throughput of data and provide a set of common rules for all hosts, whether on the ARPAnet or on other networks connected to it.

* Cerf discussed TCP with Bob Kahn, and together they specified the protocol. In September 1973 they presented it at a meeting of the INWG at the University of Sussex, where their ideas received favourable comment. Eight months later, in May 1974, the pair published a paper on TCP in the IEEE's Transactions on Communications.

* By the end of 1974 three implementations were being written in parallel: at BBN, Stanford (programmed by Richard Karp) and University College, London.

* Soon after, partly as a result of research on voice communications using packet networking, *TCP was split into two protocols: TCP – which would handle features such as flow control and recovery from lost packets – and IP (Internet Protocol)*, which would provide simple addressing and forwarding of individual packets. The protocol would henceforth be called <u>TCP/IP</u>.

BUY IT, LIKE IT

* Although obviously superior to the existing NCP, *TCP/IP took some time to be accepted as the new standard for the ARPAnet*. Europe's International Standards Organization (ISO) had already specified a new protocol for the network, called '<u>OPEN SYSTEMS INTERCONNECTION</u>' (OSI), which had already been accepted by the US government.

* However, TCP/IP was rapidly gaining favour among system administrators. Public opinion held sway, and OSI was abandoned (in practice, if not officially) as the protocol for what was increasingly coming to be called the Internet.

I choose
TCP/IP

top brass decide on TCP/IP

MILITARY MEANS

In 1980 the all-powerful US military chose TCP/IP as its preferred protocol for internetting, and in 1982 a full switch-over was made from NCP to TCP/IP

ok, I'm switching over now

the great switcheroo

THE BIG TURN-OFF

* In the middle of 1982, for one day, the Internet Configuration Control Board (ICCB), founded by Vinton Cerf and chaired by David Clark from MIT, turned off the network's ability to use NCP. This was supposed to convince host system managers that the change to TCP/IP was imminent. But the warning wasn't universally heeded, so in the autumn of 1982 the board turned off NCP for two days. And then on 1 January 1983 the network's ability to use NCP was switched off for ever. With the full introduction of TCP/IP, the global Internet we know and surf today was on its way.

HEAVY TRAFFIC

* *The success of the Internet snowballed. Daily traffic was running at well over 100 million packets*, and commercial spin-off networks abounded.

* Computer-science students who'd spent their time at university having the importance of networking etched into their psyches founded their own companies to create local-area-network hardware and software.

* In 1981 Bob Metcalfe's network company, 3Com, released a version of Unix that featured a TCP/IP capability enabling 3Com's massively popular ETHERNET to be internetted with the ARPAnet.

daily internet traffic was running at well over 100 million packets

networks are important

networking - the secret of success

SUN SHINES

* At Stanford, postgraduate students **Vinod Khosla**, **Andy Bechtolsheim** and **Scott McNealy** joined forces with Berkeley computer scientist **Bill Joy** to found SUN (named after the Stanford University Network). The new company dedicated itself to the manufacture of powerful WORKSTATIONS with built-in networking capabilities. These would satisfy the needs of academics and others who wanted desktop computers that could be linked to the Internet.

* Joy had written a TCP/IP implementation for Berkeley's version of Unix, BSD. The Sun founders were aware of the great importance of being online, and installed Joy's TCP/IP-adapted BSD on its workstations, making them highly popular in the scientific community. *By 1988, Sun had sold over a billion dollars' worth of networking workstations*.

'No future in it...'

Others in the computer industry, such as Microsoft – then a small-time software house in Seattle responsible for the IBM PC's operating system – adapted and improved their products to make them network-aware. Microsoft was desperate to climb aboard the network bandwagon and had struggled with IBM to give the second generation DOS it was developing – known as OS/2 – a networking capability. IBM, however, demurred. It didn't want its desktop computers to compete with the mainframes for which it was famous.

Deeply frustrated, Microsoft approached 3Com and the two companies developed OS/2 LAN Manager, tipped at the time to sweep the networking market by 1991. It didn't. OS/2 was a commercial failure, and OS/2 LAN Manager died with it.

Paradoxically, although Microsoft recognized the importance of networking, the company saw no future in the Internet because at that time US laws effectively banned its use for commercial interests.

you've grown!

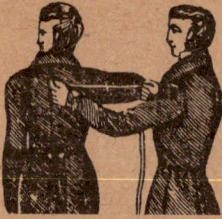

AUP RULES

In the early 1980s, all involved agreed that to open the Internet to commerce would be to bring about its downfall. To prevent the Internet being overwhelmed by commercial interests, the US National Science Foundation was charged with the task of policing the Net and enforcing a rigorous no-business strategy known as the 'Acceptable Use Policy' (AUP).

GROWTH FACTOR

* More and more networks came online and were interconnected with the Internet. In 1981 IBM created BITNET (Because It's Time NETwork), a network intended for messaging and mailing lists. The news network Usenet also came up around this time, as did many others, including the Unix network UUCP and the computer-science-community network CSNET.

SPLIT PERSONALITY

* *ARPAnet itself was split into two networks, ARPAnet and Milnet, during 1983*. Milnet was dedicated to US military traffic, while ARPAnet continued as an information exchange for academics and as a test-bed for wide-area networking theory.

* In 1986 America's National Science Foundation (NSF) established the NSFNET to provide a distributed supercomputing service to scientists and researchers, and in the following year the NSF signed a joint agreement with IBM, MCI and Merit Network Inc. to manage the Internet's backbone.

* *Control of the Internet was now out of the hands of the military* and being shared between academic and commercial interests. The Internet had grown into a

the internet was now out of the hands of the military

living, squirming thing far bigger than the sum of its constituent network parts; and **when the ARPAnet itself was switched off in 1990, few on the Net even noticed**. The ARPAnet had fulfilled its design criteria: the lines of communication remained, even though the ARPAnet had ceased to exist.

but who's it from?

internet addresses had to be memorable

* Although industry now played a large role in managing the Internet, guidelines were still in place restricting its use for commercial purposes. Indeed, the Acceptable Use Policy (AUP), which the NSF was responsible for enforcing, utterly prohibited commercial activity on the Net.

* This somewhat paradoxical state of affairs persisted until US Senator **Frederick Boucher** proposed an amendment to the law to allow the Net to 'carry a substantial volume of traffic that does not conform to the current acceptable use policy'. As a result of Boucher's amendment, the Net's virtual doors were thrown wide open.

KEY WORDS

BACKBONE:
The paths of net traffic
DNS:
Domain Name System, a system that resolves an alphanumeric Internet address (such as www.sixty3ink.co.uk) into a numerical form (255.243.17.91)

Serve you right

Vital to the Internet's growth was the method of addressing known as the Domain Name System (DNS). Prior to DNS's invention in 1983, Internet addresses were entirely numerical and almost impossible to remember. A solution was sought, and a University of Wisconsin researcher, Paul Mockapetris, provided it. In 1983 he suggested the introduction of domain name servers to resolve addresses expressed as names (composed of words or parts of words), rather than as numbers. The addresses would be constructed in a hierarchical form, using the country of origin, organization type and server name.

it's an interconnected virtual universe

A SECOND REVOLUTION

* In 1965 Theodore (Ted) Nelson presented a visionary paper to the twentieth conference of the Association of Computing Machinery, a professional body representing the American computer-science community. It was entitled 'A File Structure for the Complex, the Changing and the Intermediate'.

Ted Nelson and his visionary ideas stole the show

SURFING THE DOCUVERSE

* In his document *Nelson presented the idea of an interconnected virtual universe of text, images, sounds and animation, all of which could be retrieved and examined non-sequentially*. He called this linked universe of documents the 'DOCUVERSE', and named the overall system for manipulating it 'XANADU'.

* With Xanadu, connections between documents would be made using hypertext links – a system proposed by Doug Englebart several years earlier. In this context, 'hyper' means non-hierarchical, non-sequential, and the idea of hyperlinks is to weave related information together into a free-form virtual linked library accessible from any 'angle'.

* Perhaps because it was so ahead of its time, Ted Nelson never managed to create a working Xanadu.

KEY WORDS

HYPERLINK:
a non-linear connection that links information

MEMEX:
the hyperlink system devised in the 1940s by Vannevar Bush

XANADU:
Ted Nelson's hyperlinked multimedia virtual universe

for helpful hints, enquire within

ENQUIRE WITHIN

✱ The final and arguably greatest revolution in the development of the Net, for the time being at least, came in 1980. Its instigator was Oxford graduate **Tim Berners-Lee**, at that time an unassuming programmer at CERN, the European particle-physics laboratory, in Geneva.

✱ Berners-Lee was becoming increasingly frustrated with the way the various items of information he needed on a daily basis – his diary, list of telephone numbers and address book – were scattered over several databases on isolated networks at the laboratory, making it all but impossible for him to retrieve all of them simultaneously. The most effective way to link them together, he decided, was to use what he has since described as 'random associations between arbitrary pieces of information'.

information was scattered over isolated networks

✱ With this in mind *he developed a program using hypertext links and, somewhat whimsically, named it Enquire*, after the popular Victorian book Enquire Within Upon Everything (still in print in the 1970s) that offered helpful hints on unrelated subjects to householders.

ARGHH!

an idea ahead of its time

ENGLEBART AND NLS

Doug Englebart's hypertext document-linking system was known as the NLS (oNLine System). Although it preceded Ted Nelson's Xanadu by several years, it failed to catch on – because the technology simply wasn't available for it.

AIDE-MÉMOIRE

The hyperlinked ideas of both Doug Englebart and Ted Nelson were preceded by Dr Vannevar Bush's Memex system. Bush was a scientific advisor to US President Roosevelt during World War II. He published a paper entitled 'As We May Think', which described a system 'whereby any item may be caused at will to select immediately and automatically any other [item]'.

time to go back

TEMPTED BACK

* Soon after completing Enquire, Tim Berners-Lee left CERN to work as a network consultant; and after his departure, Enquire went largely unused at CERN. In 1989, however, he was back, tempted by the possibilities of working at what in the meantime had become Europe's largest Internet site (CERN had gone online in 1984).

Tim Berners-Lee returned to Cern in 1989

'we could look it up on the world wide web'

THE WEB GETS ITS NAME

* The problem of linking together information still intrigued him, and in March 1989 he submitted a proposal to the laboratory for an information-management system, based on hypertext, that would solve the problems associated with the hierarchical information-delivery systems used at that time.

* The new system would enable visiting scientists from around the world to get up to speed quickly on the lab's various projects. Berners-Lee wrote in his proposal that the system would provide a 'single user-interface to many large classes of stored information such as reports, notes, databases, computer documentation and online systems help'. He suggested the information-retrieval system be called the 'WORLD WIDE WEB'.

GREEN LIGHT

* *In 1990 Berners-Lee was given the go-ahead*; and, working with a small team of programmers, he developed a server to dispense information and a simple browser with which to navigate it.

* The team created the HTTP PROTOCOL (HyperText Transport Protocol), the Web server used to transmit data; HTML (HyperText Markup Language), to construct multimedia World Wide Web documents; and the URL (Uniform Resource Locator) system of addressing these documents. They then ported this software to several platforms and, in 1991, released it – to a largely unresponsive world.

FUTURISTIC

* *The World Wide Web was a remarkable leap in computer and networking technology*. But good though it was, the Web needed one more development before it would catch the attention of the world.

* That development came from a team of programmers at the University of Illinois. In 1992 postgraduate **Marc Andreesen** discovered the WWW system at CERN and decided that what was missing was a point-and-click WEB BROWSER. He wrote Mosaic (later to become Netscape Navigator), and the Web was on its way.

NEXT STEP

In 1985, silicon supremo Steve Jobs left Apple – manufacturer of the Macintosh computer – and launched NeXT, a company dedicated to revolutionizing the workstation industry using an operating system based on object-oriented principles.

WWW

multimedia

Tim Berners-Lee working with a small team of programmers developed a server to dispense information and a simple browser

?

The story of how the World Wide Web was transformed from what was essentially a text-retrieval system into the multimedia extravaganza known and loved today is told in Chapter 2.

EXPONENTIAL FUTURE

* If we can predict one sure thing about the future of the Internet it is this: that the network will continue to grow – and grow exponentially. Already, there are millions of host computers, accessed billions of times a day by ordinary people who account for trillions of databytes of traffic flowing across the network. And hundreds of thousands of new users are getting connected every month.

the internet grows minute by minute

BUSINESS BLOSSOMS

* Now that online transactions using credit cards (driven in part by the supreme success of the E-PORN industry) are more secure and more widely available, e-commerce is burgeoning – and not just those dull old sales of airline and theatre tickets and flowers that were pushed as suitable reasons for going online in the early 1980s.

* Supermarkets offer virtual browsing, accept online orders, and deliver within hours. You can buy books, clothes, specialist foods, jewellery, electronic items, pets – and even partners – on the Net.

KEY WORDS

E-COMMERCE: business conducted on the World Wide Web

can you get pineapples **On LINE?**

shop till you drop on the net

✱ But *many e-businesses simply didn't exist before the advent of widespread public access to the Net*, and some don't operate at all outside the World Wide Web (the incredibly successful Internet book shop Amazon.com is a prime example).

find your ideal
partner on the net

the internet is the
centre of many
people's existence

I LINK THEREFORE I AM

✱ *And the most amazing thing about it all? This monstrous communications revolution, this earthquake in world interconnectivity, happened almost without a murmur from the public.* No blood was shed, no government or class overthrown. The Internet arrived and with it came free, uncensored access to vast amounts of information, delivered into the hands of all who want it. It has opened up new ways of cooperating, of acquiring knowledge and exchanging and ideas. And for some people, it has practically become the centre of their existence.

THE WORLD'S YOUR OYSTER

With a connection to the Internet, you can talk to anyone in the world similarly connected, buy groceries, join political parties and pressure groups, explore some of the world's leading libraries, and tap into the news as it happens. The range of goods and services available on the Net is potentially limitless.

I give you
the internet

WOW!

CHAPTER 1
WHAT'S ON THE NET?

* The Internet is a vast universe consisting of millions of host computers, thousands of disparate networks and hundreds of different services, all woven into the virtual fabric of cyberspace and delivered to your desktop via a modem and telephone line.

the internet brings the whole universe to you

INFINITE DIVERSITY

* *Apart from the fundamental hardware, no great overall plan was used in the design of the Internet.* Networks sprang up and were connected to the original ARPAnet in response to the needs of academics, US government contractors and the military.
* With the advent of widespread public access in the early to mid 1990s, host computers on existing networks were gradually adapted to meet the requirements of those who LOGGED ON. The result is that the Internet is now enormously diverse.

VIRTUAL V. PHYSICAL

* The Internet is a virtual network consisting of thousands of interconnected physical networks with millions of host computers attached.

An *INTERNET SERVICE PROVIDER* (ISP) is your gateway into this virtual world; the software running on your machine is what accesses and manipulates the services to be found there. Some services, such as the newsgroup network USENET, are dedicated networks in their own right, whereas others are specific applications available from general networks.

did you hear you can do it on the phone?

it's all delivered by a phone line

were there any instructions?

the internet is mainly unregulated

The Internet software running on your computer brings these services to you and interprets them for you. Run an Archie client and you'll access Archie servers, fire up a World Wide Web browser and Web pages will appear on your screen.

* Today, the Internet is dominated by three services: EMAIL, the WORLD WIDE WEB and USENET, though there are many others. FTP, IRC, Gopher and Telnet – we'll take a closer look at some of the more popular services later in the book. But for now, let's have a brief glimpse of what's available on the Net.

INVISIBLE NETWORKS

To you and other users, the networks and to a lesser extent the host computers connected to them will be almost entirely invisible – a major objective in Internet design. Connect your desktop computer to the Internet and all you'll see is the service you've chosen to access.

we aim to be invisible

networks are designed to be invisible to users

WHAT'S IN A NAME?

* Each Internet service is denoted by its address, or Uniform Resource Locator (URL). It is the Net's standard method of specifying the protocol, network, host address and data type used in retrieving an element from cyberspace.

Mmmm....

pondering on name

thinking of a good name can be a trial

WEB ADDRESSES

* For example, the URL of a typical Web page will be something like this:

http://www.wimpleware.co.uk/home.html

This looks rather daunting, but is simply saying that:

* The file's name is 'home' (indicating that it is a 'home page')
* It is written in HTML (the programming language used to create Web pages)
* It is stored on the World Wide Web server known as 'wimpleware', which is a commercial server (.co) based in the United Kingdom (.uk)
* The method used for shunting the file around the Internet is HyperText Transport Protocol (http).

The part of the address giving the server's name, type and country is called the 'domain name'.

KEY WORDS

DOMAIN:
Part of a host's URL which specifies its type and location

SERVER:
A host computer that provides a service on the Internet (such as FTP) to other computers (clients)

URL:
Uniform Resource Locator, the standard address for an element in cyberspace

type carelessly at your peril

WHAT'S IN A URL?

✱ Only countries outside the United States are noted in the domain name: .uk, .jp, .fr and so on. Domain names also specify the type of organization responsible for the server – such as .com (US) or .co (rest of the world) for a commercial server, .edu (US) and .ac (rest of world) for an academic institute such as a university, .gov for governments, and so on.

names can give plenty away

✱ Among the many other designations used in URLs are ftp:// for file servers, gopher:// for Gopherspace servers, and http:// for secure http servers. Gopherspace, FTP and the others are all discussed later in this chapter.

PUNCTILIOUS TYPING

✱ Some URLs can be pretty complex, and it's a must that you type them correctly – including all punctuation – if the Net's domain name server is to resolve the address correctly. Email addresses aren't case-sensitive, but URLs are – so typing **hTTP://Www.WimpLewaRe.Co.UK/HOME.htMl** might have unpredictable results.

✱ Always ensure that you type an oblique (/), rather than a backslash (\). Also, it's useful to know that some URLs contain the addresses of subdirectories on servers running the Unix operating system - a fact denoted by a tilde (~), like this:

http://www.wimpleware.co.uk/~jerry/mybook.html Which means that the HTML file 'mybook' is stored in a subdirectory called 'jerry'.

UNIX V. DOS

Occasionally, you'll see .htm in place of .html. The former means that the file is stored on a PC server running the DOS operating system, whereas the latter indicates a file stored on a Unix server. DOS has a strict naming convention with a maximum of eight characters followed by a maximum of three characters. Unix has no such restrictions.

but the conventions are very strict

tell me about
email grandad

MAIL MODEL

*** Electronic mail (email)
can claim to be the great-
grandparent of all Internet
services, since it was
used on the Net before
any other services
existed. In fact it even
predates the Internet,
having been used on the
world's first wide-area
packet-switched network, with just four hosts
connected to four IMPs (see Introduction).**

email was the grandfather
of all things

EXPRESS MESSAGES

* *Email quickly became the fledgling
network's fastest growing source of traffic*,
as academics all around the United States
communicated with each other and shared
data almost instantly. Today, email is by far
the most used Internet facility.

* The first public use of email came in the
early 1980s, when personal computers and
BULLETIN BOARD services (BBSs) became
popular. Bulletin board software transforms a
personal computer into a kind of host
machine on a network.

* Other computer users can dial into the
bulletin board using a standard telephone
line and a modem, log on and leave
messages, post mail to other users,
download files, play games, and so on.

Geeks do their bit

*The success of hobbyist
bulletin boards prompted
the founding of several
large commercial services
such as Compuserve,
Delphi and BIX in the
United States and CIX in
the UK, all offering email
as standard.*

is the poor old
postie second best?

SNAIL MAIL SUPERSEDED

I've been superseded

✻ The idea of email caught on quickly. Now you no longer needed to go out and post a letter. Nor was it necessary to wait several days for it to reach its destination. By mailing it electronically via your computer, your missive would reach its destination almost instantly, and could be read by the recipient and responded to equally quickly.

✻ Unfortunately, email only worked if both the sender and receiver were signed up to the same service – the same hobbyist or public-access BBS – or if their machines were physically connected (for example, via a LAN inside the same office building). With the rise in public Internet access, however, email came into its own.

MESSAGE IN A BOTTLE

✻ *Today it no longer matters who you're signed up with*, because ultimately all ISPs are attached to the Internet and anyone can email anyone else on the Net, anywhere in the world. Nor is it used only for sending plain-text messages. You can also email 'ATTACHMENTS' such as data files, graphics and even programs, though these have to be encoded by the sending machine and decoded at the receiving end.

KEY WORDS

ATTACHMENTS: images, programs, word-processor files or other items attached to an email message

BBS: Bulletin Board Service, a kind of single-access network for personal computers (BBS software transforms a desktop computer into a host when connected to a telephone line via a modem)

if only I had email

it no longer matters where in the world you are – messages can get to you

ELECTRONIC PINBOARDS

* Another early Internet service that predated the Internet as a virtual network - and still one of the most popular - is Usenet, the newsgroup service.

Usenet -
thousands of
virtual pinboards

look on Usenet for anything from fish fanciers to admirers of the male and female form

OMNIUM-GATHERUM

* Imagine a pinboard at a college or at work. People pin up messages, 'For Sale' notices, and so on. Then other people come along and read them, and perhaps pin up a message of their own in response. Occasionally two individuals might communicate directly after reading each other's postings on the pinboard. Now imagine thousands of pinboards stored electronically on servers around the world, all available to be posted and read at any time of the day or night by anyone, anywhere. That, essentially, is Usenet.

* _Think of almost any subject under the sun that interests you, and there'll be an active Usenet newsgroup devoted to it_, with interested people contributing anecdotes, help, advice, questions, or 'For Sale' and 'Wanted' notices. From radio hams to classic car enthusiasts they're all there, strutting their stuff on Usenet.

FLAMES OF WRATH

✱ ABUSE – known as 'flame wars' or 'being flamed' – plays its part, too. FLAMING used to be reserved for those trying to advertise commercial services in the days of a non-commercial Internet; or for newbies who asked questions on subjects that had already been answered many times previously in the same newsgroup (the answers to which were therefore readily available from newsgroup archives).

✱ Nowadays, with the global take-up of the Internet, those who consider themselves an intellectual elite – computer geeks, American college professors, and the like – are very much in the minority on Usenet. People who post to Usenet are more likely to be ordinary men and women with a question to ask or an answer to contribute. The result is far fewer flamings.

Fun and Games?

From time to time mischievous individuals try to incite flame wars by making provocative postings, but the tactic hardly ever works – few can be bothered to respond.

newbies bore me rigid

tedious postings are usually ignored

GOTCHA!

flamings are fewer these days

NO STONE UNTURNED

Mailing lists and newsgroups are similar approaches to the same end – the provision of interactive discussion groups covering every possible topic you can think of and some you most definitely can't (and perhaps wouldn't want to).

dazzling!

THE WORLD WIDE WEB

* If email is the Internet's most used service, then the World Wide Web is its most familiar. The WWW is the Internet's friendliest face, a multimedia experience of hyperlinked pages featuring often dazzling text, graphics, sounds and animation, all easily accessed using a point-and-click browser.

...and that's before breakfas

KEY WORDS

MULTIMEDIA:
still or moving images, sounds and text combined electronically

SPECIAL AKA

Whether it's referred to as the World Wide Web, WWW, or simply the Web, and its components as Web sites, websites, sites or pages, all refer to the same globally hyperlinked network of multimedia pages.

I've been to Nebraska, Tasmania and Bogota...

the web is a veritable aladdin's cave of goodies

do you know honey, it was an unforgettable experience

UNFORGETTABLE, THAT'S WHAT YOU ARE

* *Some sites feature all of these things, others offer little more than plain text and perhaps a few hyperlinks* – but whatever is available at the sites you access, the

experience of surfing the Web is an unforgettable one.

* The World Wide Web is simple to use and yet an extremely POWERFUL TOOL for those who want easy access to hard information. Almost all government agencies, public bodies and the media consider a presence on the Web essential – though many have yet to realize what makes for a good site (it's not enough simply to be there); and nowadays thousands of small businesses advertise their wares on the Web, many of them providing online shopping at a click of a mouse.

* What's more, millions of individuals around the world have put up their own Web site, usually in support of a hobby such as wine making, hang gliding or collecting, but often simply to weave themselves into a tiny part of cyberspace. 'Hi, I'm Randy!' could open up a world of erotic possibility, or simply be the home page of Randy Kowalski of Wichita Falls, Nebraska.

COOL

so much about **wine making**

the net is cyber heaven for hobbyists of all kinds

Hi, I'm Randy!

if you want to meet Randy - get on line!

FIRST AMONG EQUALS

Increasingly the Web is replacing – or at least offering an alternative to – many of the traditional services such as email, newsgroups and file download, all of which can be accessed via its pages. Services such as Archie are now accessed almost entirely via the Web.

it's all free
(for a while)

FILES FOR FREE

*** No doubt from philanthropic
motives, many computer-systems
managers make tens, sometimes
hundreds, of megabytes of
hard-drive space on their
computers available to
store shareware and PD
software for free public
access and download. This is
achieved using a method of data
transfer known as 'FTP', or
sometimes as 'anonymous FTP'.**

shareware has a free trial
period, then you have to
start paying

NO KNOWLEDGE NEEDED

* As with many other services, *only a
passing familiarity with the technology is
required* to make use of FTP, because all
the hard work is done by the software. All
you have to do is point your FTP 'client' at
an FTP server, navigate the site's
directories to locate the stuff you want,
then click on the files and download them
to your computer. Some of the stuff you'll
find is shareware, most of it is in the
public domain, and all of it is potentially
useful to you.

* The FTP client software is available as
shareware from a variety of sources on the
Internet (ISPs usually maintain a selection
of popular tools for download by their
customers). There are versions for both

PCs and Macs, and a variety of operating systems including Windows and Unix. Two of the most popular are the Windows client WS_FTP, and Fetch for the Macintosh (sources for both are given in the Appendix). The Unix operating system has an FTP client 'built in' – you simply type 'ftp' and the relevant server name when prompted to do so.

REMOTE WORKER

✱ *The client programs are designed to negotiate a connection with a remote FTP server*, using your email address as a log-in name and the word 'guest' as a password (FTP is 'anonymous' in that you don't have to have an account on the server in order to log on). You will then be presented with a list of directories and files.

you choose first; you're the guest

with FTP, you are a guest

✱ *Navigating these will be child's play for anyone even vaguely familiar with a GUI operating system*, such as Windows or the Apple Mac's system and finder.

TO AND FRO

FTP is used to upload files as well as download them. Some FTP servers feature a special upload directory.

easy peasy

using FTP is child's play

WHAT EXACTLY IS FTP?

FTP (File Transfer Protocol) is the name of the protocol involved in downloading files. It negotiates a connection with the remote server, transfers the files and checks them for errors. The acronym is now also used as a catch-all description of the process, as in 'I'm FTPing this file from site xyz'.

57

DOWNLOADING WITH FTP

* Two types of download are available. Text is transferred in the form of simple ASCII files, but programs are transferred as binary files to make sure they remain 'runnable'.

deciding on downloading can be tough - let someone else decide

Choosing between the two downloading methods is not usually necessary, because the client will attempt to choose for you.

WHAT TO CHOOSE

* If you do have to make a choice, text files will probably have the filename extender '.TXT' and PC binary files will be labelled '.EXE' or '.COM'. Still others will be compressed binary files with extenders such as '.ZIP' and '.LHA'.

RUSH HOUR

* *Some of the more popular dedicated FTP servers have a startling amount of traffic going through them*, so you may find it difficult to connect or that the transfer takes place as a trickle. Non-dedicated FTP servers are often limited to perhaps a few tens of ANONYMOUS VISITORS at a time, and maybe even less than ten.

KEY WORDS

APPLICATION:
a computer program such as a word processor

ASCII
American Standard Code for Information Interchange, standard way of specifying alphanumeric and certain other characters

BINARY FILES:
computer programs (as opposed to text or image files)

DEDICATED SERVER:
a server devoted to performing one task

* The trick is to be patient and to take into account the waking and sleeping times of users in other countries. If you're in the UK, the best time to access a server in the US is early to mid morning – ideally on Saturday or Sunday, to get the benefit of cheap-rate phone calls.

try to avoid
rush hour on
the net

your ISP will keep
useful tools for you

TOOL BOX

All of the software tools necessary to access the Internet's services are available free from FTP sites – though it's something of a chicken-and-egg situation, since to get to them you need to be able to log on to and use the Internet. Often your own ISP will keep a selection of the most popular applications and Net tools to save you the effort of finding them.

FREE FOR ALL

Public-domain applications (aka PD, freeware, giftware etc.) are software that has been given away free by programmers. You don't have to pay to acquire or use them, but copyright notices and certain text files containing author information must not be discarded or changed. SHAREWARE software you can acquire for free, but you pay a fee if you continue to use the software after a trial period. Some of the most amazing software available can be had free or very cheaply from the Net – including the world's most popular Web browser, NETSCAPE NAVIGATOR.

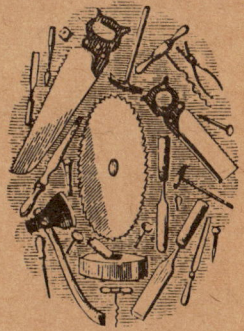

pick your time to
go on line

ACCESSING INFORMATION

* Devised by programmers Paul Lindner and Mark McCahill at the University of Minnesota at the end of the 1980s, Gopher is an Internet service devoted to providing access to filed information, rather than actual

finding information is easier on the net

files. Gopher servers (often simply called Gophers) are linked together, and the resulting mass of linked information is known as Gopherspace. On Gopher servers, information is organized under menus.

Web rat

Gopherspace is still out there and you can access it using a dedicated Gopher client or a gateway from the Web. It still offers a lot of quality information, too, though mainly of an academic nature.

'could I see the menu please?'

OUTSHONE BY THE WEB

* *Formerly extremely popular, Gopher has now more or less fallen from grace*, for two very good reasons. Someone has to organize and catalogue data on Gopher servers – once a relatively easy task, but now almost impossible given the SHEER SCALE OF DATA available on the Net. But perhaps a more important factor has been the phenomenal success of the World Wide Web. The Web does pretty much everything that Gopher can do, and a whole lot more; and the Web's multimedia pages are much more seductive than Gopher's text menus.

FIND FILE

✻ Being able to download files for free using anonymous FTP is fantastic, but first you have to know where to find them. One way to do that is by using ARCHIE, a Net-wide search system devised at Canada's McGill University. Archie queries special Archie servers, which feature extensive catalogues of downloadable files stored at FTP sites.

gopher servers are linked together to make gopherspace

✻ *Archie servers are accessed using an Archie client program* such as WS_Archie for the PC. To start a search, connect to your ISP, run the Archie client, then select an Archie server from those available (try to choose one that's close to you).

✻ Specify a search pattern (most often, the name of the file you're trying to find). Select from a range of search types, such as case-sensitive, substring, and so on. Indicate the number of results matching the search pattern you'd like to scan (fewer is quicker), then set Archie going by clicking on the search (or submit or start) button.

Hello Archie

Like many other classic Internet services, Archie can now be accessed via the Web. A number of Archie servers are listed on page 188. To use one, point your browser at it, type in your search pattern, click on submit, and the server will do the rest.

ummm, duh

you can get very silly answers from archie

I'm surprised it even exists

THE DIRECT APPROACH

* Trust is a fragile thing. Given the sensational news stories about computer hackers, worms, viruses and the like regularly broadcast during the fifteen years or so the popular media has understood the notion of computing, it's a wonder that an open-architecture communications medium such as the Internet exists at all.

NEWS

hackers, worms and viruses on WWW

the internet is a mine of sensational and scary stories

OPEN ACCESS

* It's therefore all the more remarkable that many hosts not only make Web sites, FTP servers and other services available to anyone with a computer and modem, but also throw wide their silicon doors and allow you to log on and manipulate their machines as if you were sitting at a terminal connected to them directly.

* *This practice is called 'telnetting'*, and it's a legacy of days gone by when users of Unix computers would telnet into each other's machines to access data.

THRILLING INTERFACE

* A telnet connection is a text-only one. What you'll see is a LOG-ON PROMPT, followed by a request for a PASSWORD, then perhaps a menu of options leading to screens of text.

we've got a virus

✱ If you've telnetted into a Unix system, all you'll see is a shell prompt and you'll probably have to use some of the standard Unix UTILITIES, such as finger (to locate a particular user), or OS commands such as ls, cd, cat, pwd and so on. Thrilling stuff for those weaned on a windowing environment!

✱ What you can do when you make a telnet connection depends upon the PRIVILEGES assigned to the account you've telnetted into.

be my guest come on in

✱ Telnetting is achieved using a telnet client (what else?). This can be a dedicated client such as Telnet, which comes with Windows, or NCSA Telnet for the Mac. Or it can take the form of terminal software offering VT100 or VT52 compatibility (to transform your all-singing modern machine into a dumb terminal!), such as the bundled Windows application HyperTerminal or Zterm for the Mac.

anyone is welcome on telnet

MAKING FRIENDS

With a burning desire to explore a particular host but no legitimate account, you might be able to email a friendly systems manager and persuade him/her to provide you with one. Geeks are usually pretty friendly towards the genuinely interested.

Play time

Nowadays telnet is primarily used to access online multi-user games (MUGs), or to research experimental operating systems such as Minix (a Unix look-alike), or to log into a library system or government department that has information to disseminate but hasn't got its own Web page.

SHUT THE DOOR

When you've finished with a telnet connection, be sure to log out properly – otherwise the host machine will waste time trying to service a client that has long since disappeared. Not a big deal, but good 'netiquette' anyway.

CHANNEL CROSSING

I need a good chat

* Always a big source of traffic, personal communications of various kinds play an enormous part in Net throughput. There's email of course, but many choose an even more immediate method of communication known as Internet Relay Chat (IRC).

IRC is just like chatting on the phone

CHIT-CHAT

KEY WORDS

CHANNEL:
a line of communication for users of IRC

IRC:
Internet Relay Chat, typed real-time conversations over the Internet

* *IRC is a real-time communications protocol that enables users to chat much as they would on the phone* – but instead of talking, the conversation is typed.
* IRC conversations take place via 'CHANNELS' (denoted by a hash character such as #newbie) that are provided by IRC servers, much as FTP is offered by FTP servers.

WASTE OF TIME?

we should meet

you can talk for hours to people with similar interests

* All of which sounds like an easy and cheap way to communicate with friends and family who are remote. But it isn't. IRC is really just another way to waste endless hours at the keyboard. It's ENTERTAINMENT (well...) of a kind, rather like CB radio once was.

✱ There's a lot of virtual shouting and a lot of weird people who fib about who they are, where they come from and what they do – though they may be telling the truth about what it is they want to do to you! Of course, IRC can be a quick and convenient way to hold interesting conversations with people with like-minded interests. But usually it's just prattle for an idle hour.

tee hee

according to an old Internet joke, on the Net no one knows you're a dog

most of what happens on IRC is idle chat

UNDER COVER

According to an old Internet joke, on the Net no one knows you're a dog. Which pretty much describes IRC. Some users adopt all kinds of weird and wacky personalities, and the truth can be almost impossible to discover.

✱ Also, *be aware that you might not be conversing with a real person*. Software robots (known as 'bots' in IRC-speak) are automated interactive chatterers that can be rather more lifelike than some of the real users. And, of course, the converse might also be true – someone claiming to be a bot may actually be human!

DO YOU SPEAK IRC?

/ADMIN	server displays server information
/CLEAR	clears your screen
/TIME	displays the current time (and date)
/WHO	list all channel users

DIVE IN

* To make use of IRC, you'll need the IRC client software, which can be had as freeware or shareware. Windows 95 users should seek out mIRC, and there's Ircle for the Apple Macintosh (see Appendix). Windows 98 is shipped complete with an IRC client called Microsoft Chat.

I'm giving
IRC a try

TALK TIME

* *With your connection to the Internet up and running, start the IRC software and select a suitable IRC server.* Try to locate one which is geographically close to you. That way you'll limit delays in sending and receiving messages.

* Once connected, type /list to see a list of available channels and what it is they're discussing. When you find one you want to interact with, type /nick plus a nickname to protect your identity, followed by /join #channel.

* Alternatively, if there isn't a channel already devoted to your interests, type /join plus a new channel name (preceded by a #) to start your own channel.

* When you join a channel, existing users

I never
knew that

every hobby is catered
for on IRC

will be sent a message such as 'Scooby has joined channel #Cartoons', so that everyone knows you've arrived. You'll either be greeted or ignored. Read what you find there, follow the conversations, and offer your own thoughts. When you've had enough, type /leave or /quit. If you thought the Net was littered with unnecessary jargon, just wait until you join an IRC channel!

SAFETY FIRST

✱ Internet Relay Chat, much like any other open communications medium, should be used with CAUTION. Don't give out personal details, which could be used to find out who you are or where you live (some pretty off-the-wall characters are lurking in the IRC shadows). Though guidelines exist for safe and polite chatting, they're largely ignored. If you don't like the look of a particular channel, move on to another or start your own.

TAKE NO NOTICE

✱ *You can complain to the server owners about unpleasant IRC users*, but it's generally more effective to ignore them. And don't respond in kind, unless you want to spend an hour blowing off steam – otherwise you'll be falling right into the hands of the abusive.

don't give out any personal details, especially not your address

SWOT UP RE IRC

Discover the gory details of IRC by pointing your browser at http://www.kei.com/irc.html

try not to get involved in arguments

CHAPTER 2

THE WORLD OF THE WEB

* The World Wide Web (alias WWW, the Web or W3) is a hyperlinked interactive virtual universe that rolls together text and graphics, sounds and animation into a gigantic multimedia extravaganza, the like of which no one had ever experienced before.

HYPE AND HYPERLINKS

That's the hype, here's the nitty-gritty. The World Wide Web is a global virtual network of 'pages' created using HyperText Markup Language (HTML). This special programming language, devised specifically for constructing Web documents, makes it easy to create live links to objects elsewhere on the page or on pages held at other sites on the network. HTML is also used to style text, position pictures and specify backdrops. Web-page links are navigated by clicking on them. Whereupon they're activated – and either whatever it is they're linked to appears on your screen or you are whisked to another page.

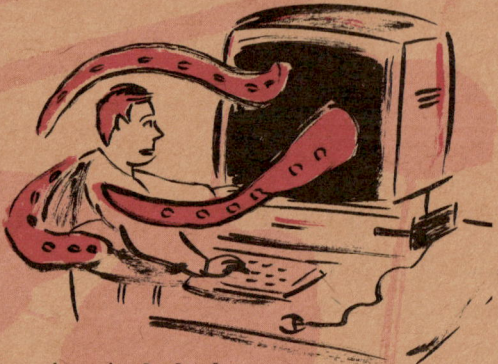

the web slowly drags
you into its clutches

WHAT YOU GET

* At least, that's what you've heard. The reality is all of that and none of it. True, many of the Web's millions of pages feature super sounds and graphics, cute animated cartoons, and information by the bucket-load. But *the Web can be a bewildering place for the uninitiated, and a distinct disappointment for the non-techie first-time user* preprimed with lashings of hype.

* In fact, the Web is a slow-burn experience that slowly wraps its virtual tendrils around you and draws you in – so that almost without knowing it, you're frantically clicking ahead, hither and thither, now at a site in Iceland, now jumping via a hyperlink to one in Japan, then trawling through a flea-bitten banana republic's crop-yield figures for 1995, before free-falling onto some redneck Texan's home page devoted to a love affair with the horse and the pick-up truck. And all from the safety of your own mouse and monitor.

hang on, I'm just checking on banana sales

before you know it you're hooked

SOMETHING FOR EVERYONE

✳ The Web offers a whole planet's worth of information cleverly linked together into an object-oriented experience that becomes easier and more seductive every time you use it. Whatever your interests and hobbies, professional needs or leisure requirements, somewhere on the Web, someone feels the same way and has devoted a Web site to it.

TAGGING WITH HTML

The HyperText Markup Language works by using a system of 'tags' that tell a Web browser how to interpret and display what follows. They look like this:

<HI>This is a Web page heading</HI>

Writing HTML is not especially difficult, but it is time-consuming and many HTML programmers use an HTML editor program, which does for Web pages what desktop-publishing software does for the printed page. Using it simplifies programming, enabling the programmer to concentrate on the look and feel of the Web page, instead of labouring with tags.

GETTING AROUND

* How do you navigate the Web's many pages? By using a browser program. Initially able to display only text but now fully GUI-based, Web browsers perform several functions. As well as navigating sites on the Web - which they do by using HyperText Transfer Protocol (HTTP) and URLs - they translate the HTML to be found there into styled text, plus pictures and sound.

everybody's
gone surfin'

SURFING THE WEB

* NAVIGATING through Web sites, jumping via hyperlink from one page to another, is called 'surfing the Web' or simply 'SURFING'.
* A Web browser enables you to save or print information from a Web site. It also maintains a record of sites you've visited recently, enabling you to move 'backward'

KEY WORDS

GUI:
Graphical User Interface, a computer operating system that features on-screen windows and the like controlled by a mouse and pointer
HTTP:
HyperText Transport Protocol, the protocol used to transmit hypertext Web pages over the Internet so that their multimedia contents remain intact

if only
we could
share

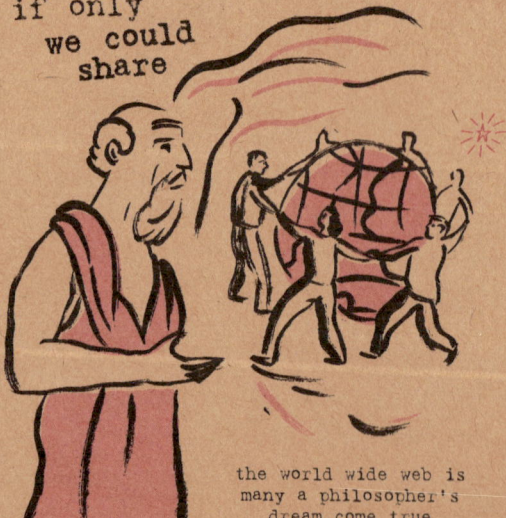

the world wide web is
many a philosopher's
dream come true

it's got a bit
out of control

the web is
largely
uncontrolled
and uncensored

POWER TO THE
PEOPLE

POWER TO THE PEOPLE

Several bodies attempt to control the Internet, to set its standards and guide its evolution. But they've had very little real effect. A far more powerful force in Web evolution has been the porn industry which probably accounts for more traffic than all other sources and has driven forward innovations such as streaming sound and video, secure credit-card transactions and shopping-cart technology.

POTENT ANARCHY

Reasons for the Web's success are manifold, though two stand out in particular: the fact that no one owns the Web and that there is little or no censorship. Unimpeded by borders, financial barriers, political allegiance and religious creeds, the Web transcends man-made boundaries to facilitate nothing more complicated than communications between anyone, anywhere, who can get access to a computer and modem.

and 'forward' through them. What's more, the Web browser can be used as a database of your FAVOURITE sites. So when you're visiting one you particularly like, simply add its URL to the browser's database – and then when you want to return to it in the future, all you need do is select it from the favourite-site list.

✱ Together, the World Wide Web and a Web browser represent the fulfilment of a vision shared by a distinguished array of computer scientists, philosophers, literary figures and others over the past 50 years or so – the concept of a virtual universe of linked object-oriented documents. Indeed, it's fair to say that that vision is now a reality: the 'docuverse' (see page 40) dreamed of by Ted Nelson, Doug Englebart and Vannevar Bush is here.

BIRTH OF A BROWSER

* We've seen (in the Introduction) how unassuming CERN programmer Tim Berners-Lee, impressed by the object-oriented interface of the NeXT computer, invented a protocol that would behave in a similar way across the burgeoning Internet, and named his invention the World Wide Web.

he's such a
dish

a really special chef was needed
to stir the final mix

STIRRING IT UP

* *Though an extremely powerful idea, the World Wide Web protocol languished at first*, because of its text-only interface. Easy for computer scientists and programmers to use, a text interface can be daunting for the non-technical – the very people who have accounted for the massive rise in Internet access. The ingredients were available, but they needed yet another chef to stir them into a tempting dish.

LOVE AT FIRST SIGHT

* In 1992 **Marc Andreessen** was a postgraduate student at the University of Illinois at Urbana-Champaign (UIUC), which had been one of the first nodes on the fledgling Internet in the early 1970s. Renowned for being at the FOREFRONT of computer science, the university ran a distributed supercomputer service, the National Centre for Supercomputer Applications (NCSA), that offered the world's scientists access to Cray computers – the fastest available. The NCSA service was maintained by an itinerant group of lecturers and postgraduate students, among them Andreessen.

* *The story goes that trawling the Net one day, Andreessen came across Tim Berners-Lee's World Wide Web*, was immediately captivated by it and instantly recognized its one real shortcoming – the lack of a Web browser with a graphical interface. Together with some student friends, he determined to write one. The result was a point-and-click browser which they called Mosaic for X (X being the GUI front-end used on computers running the Unix and Linux operating systems).

eureka!
I know what's missing

Andreessen saw the need for a web browser with a graphical interface

More Mosaic

Andreessen ported his GUI-based Mosaic browser to the PC and Apple Macintosh, and then made it available free for download by anyone on the Net. Within a year there were a million users worldwide.

'I am determined to write it...'

yipeee
I've done it

FROM MOSAIC TO NAVIGATOR

* Mosaic was destined to be a truly astounding success, though Andreessen little realized it at the time. Applications written by UIUC students were automatically the property of the university - and it would appear that Andreessen and the others were happy simply to have written something that was successful, and didn't appreciate the enormous scale of its commercial potential.

Andreessen
was happy
to be
successful

KEY WORDS

DOWNLOAD:
to copy a program
or text file from one
machine to another
over a network

INFECTIOUS ENTHUSIASM

* At that point **Jim Clarke**, founder of Stanford high-tech company SGI, appeared on the scene. Recently retired from SGI, Clarke was casting about for a fresh project. In the meantime, Marc Andreessen had left UIUC and been hired by a small software company in Silicon Valley. Aware of Mosaic's success and the programmer's recent arrival on the West Coast, Clarke sought out Andreessen and was impressed by the younger man's enthusiasm for the browser. He decided to gather together the entire team that had devised the program and found a new company, Mosaic Communications Corp., to market it.

* *The pair flew to Illinois and were able to recruit five of the original seven programmers* (with Andreessen himself making a sixth). The seventh,

the team was
reassembled along
with Andreessen

Chris Wilson, had been employed by Microsoft and had no wish to give up a safe seat at the software giant for a shaky one in a fledgling company.

Netscape Navigator was nicknamed Mozilla

✱ The new company's first task was to approach UIUC for the <u>RIGHTS</u> to market Mosaic. This, they assumed, would be a mere formality. To their surprise, the university refused to relinquish the name Mosaic and could not be shifted. Programming talent not exactly being in short supply among them, however, they promptly rewrote their browser and dubbed it <u>MOZILLA</u> – though its commercial name (which reflected their company's new name) would be Netscape Navigator.

LEGENDARY REVENGE

✱ Although its commercial name is Navigator, Netscape's browser has always been known in-house as 'Mozilla' – *a reference to its mission to chew up and spit out Mosaic*.

Masterly marketing

The really clever part of the project was the marketing. Rather than trying to sell the program in the traditional way, Netscape made it available as a shareware download over the Net. Home users could use and enjoy it without having to stump up, while business users had to pay a (relatively small) fee after a trial period. It was a master stroke. The browser market exploded, and within 18 months Netscape Navigator became, in Jim Clarke's own words, the 'most rapidly assimilated product in history', with an installed user base of 65 million people. According to Clarke, 'No one had ever achieved an installed base of 65 million anything – except perhaps Microsoft.' And not surprisingly, Microsoft was hardly likely to let success like that pass it by.

'but no one has ever achieved an installed base of 65 million dear'

it's microsoft explorer
I presume

FROM MSN TO EXPLORER

✱ While Netscape's Navigator marched inexorably into the homes, offices and colleges of the world's online community, Microsoft continued to flog a value-added dead horse, the Microsoft Network (MSN).

ENTER EXPLORER

microsoft started to explore new territory

✱ An essentially closed network utilizing proprietary protocols, MSN was Microsoft's vision of a connected future. Not for the first or the last time, however, Microsoft had underestimated the power of the Internet and its vast universe of users.

✱ It became obvious to Microsoft that if it were to check the rise of Netscape and certain other Internet-oriented companies, it would need to scramble aboard the e-gravy train sooner rather than later.

✱ The company therefore launched its own browser, INTERNET EXPLORER. Although Explorer had much of the look and feel of Navigator, there was one important difference – Microsoft decided to give it away absolutely FREE to anyone who wanted it, from the lowliest home micro user to the largest corporate business. By doing so, they would

NECK AND NECK

Whatever Net users feel about Microsoft, there's no doubt that Internet Explorer is a powerful browser and one that's packed with features. The geek consensus is that Navigator just has the edge powerwise – but if that is so, then Explorer ranks second by only the slimmest of slim margins.

be able to break Netscape's hold on the market and win back the attention of the increasing numbers of online computer users.

FREEBIES FOR NETIZENS

✱ In the years following the launch of Internet Explorer, Microsoft became the subject of litigation (at present still unresolved) alleging that it had gained too much control of a powerful market and was spoiling the market for other companies by giving its products away for free in the fight for an installed user base (in other words, you!).

✱ And for Net users, there's another benefit of the browser war. The intense

they have too much control

microsoft are still the subject of litigation

EXPLORER V. NAVIGATOR

Until recently Navigator had far more followers than Explorer – but with the release of IE 4.0, Microsoft produced a browser that matched or bettered the competition. Paradoxically, given its immense lead, Navigator has switched its strategy from being an all-in-one browser with mail and news facilities in the same application (version 3.0), to become a suite of programs under the umbrella name Netscape Communicator. There are now individual programs for news, mail and the Web, each selected from a menu bar, which is much closer to the way Explorer handles the various Net services.

netscape has to be the best

no!

the browser war has benefits for the user

competition has led to innovation on a timescale that is hard to believe. Updates for major software packages are released quarterly on average, and are free to Netizens eager to act as BETA TESTERS.

USING NAVIGATOR

* Whether you're using Netscape Navigator on an Apple Macintosh or a PC, the program's interface and operation is much the same. You launch the application by double-clicking on its icon, whereupon it opens to display a standard window with a menu bar, various tool bars and a Location field in which you can enter URLs.

KEY WORDS

BOOKMARKS:
Navigator's name for favourite URLs

EMBEDDED:
a URL link within a web page

SEARCH ENGINE:
Web services which perform keyword searches of the Web

Bookmarks

After surfing for a while, you'll probably discover Web sites that you'd like to visit again. Navigator offers a system of 'bookmarks' for storing the URLs of your favourite sites. From the menu bar, click Bookmarks and select Add Bookmark. Now when you access the Bookmarks menu, it will display those you've stored.

SURF'S UP!

* Once started, the program will access and display Netscape's own home page in the main window, unless you elect to have it start with a different home page. At this point, you can either type a new URL into the Location field or simply click a link and start surfing.

* Links are denoted by COLOUR (usually blue) and an underline. Moving the pointer over a link changes the pointer and causes the embedded URL associated with the link to be displayed at the bottom of Navigator's window. Move the pointer away from the link if you don't want to access its associated URL.

bookmarks are a useful way of finding the way back to your favourite sites

* If you click on a link then change your mind, click the STOP button. To access a previous site, click the BACK button; then, after hopping back by one or more sites, you can click the FORWARD button to return to where you were. Click the HOME button to return to Netscape's Web site (or whichever site you've chosen as the home page). When accessing links, the 'N' icon in the upper right corner will be animated to let you know the browser is actively at work.

whichever browser you choose - make it work for you

it's great to be at home

you can instruct the browser to start at your own home page

CHOOSING A HOME PAGE

* If you create your own home page or prefer the browser to start at a site you use often (a search engine, for example), *select Preferences from the Options menu, then click the Styles tab and click in the 'Start with' field*. Type the address of the new home page and click 'OK'. Next time you start the browser, it will go to the new home page.

BROWSER NUTS AND BOLTS

For straightforward surfing, there's little to choose between Netscape Navigator and Internet Explorer – though there are fans of each who would die before allowing themselves to use the other. Both of them feature menus of facilities, and both offer icons and buttons as shortcuts to the ones people tend to use most. Both sport an animated icon in the top right corner that indicates when the browser is downloading a site from the Web, so you can tell that something is happening. And both feature a range of information along the bottom of the browser window.

USING EXPLORER

* Not surprisingly, Internet Explorer operates in much the same way as Navigator. You launch the program with a double-click. Once opened, it accesses the Microsoft home page (unless you choose a different home page setting) and displays what it finds there in a standard window.

KEY WORDS

FAVORITES:
Explorer's name for the URLs of your favourite sites (what Navigator calls 'bookmarks')

'it's all so exciting on the net!'

NAME GAME

Netscape's terminology – bookmarks, links and so on – tends to be used more than Explorer's version because of Netscape's greater Net penetration

Explorer can take you straight to your favourite places

GADDING ABOUT

* Links ('shortcuts' in Explorer jargon) appear exactly as they would in Navigator and operate in precisely the same way. To browse using a link, move the mouse pointer over it, whereupon the pointer changes and the EMBEDDED URL is displayed in the lower left corner of the window.

* Click the link, and the 'e' icon in the upper right corner becomes animated to show that the program is active. Click the STOP button if you change your mind. Alternatively, you can type a URL into the Address field in the upper part of the window. For a list of sites you've visited recently, click the Address field's tab (at its right).

'just point and click if you want to stop'

YOUR FAVORITE THINGS

* Explorer organizes favourite URLs under the FAVORITES menu (the menu title is spelled US-style). Simply select Add to Favorites to store the URL of the Web page the browser is currently displaying.

* Explorer's Back and Forward buttons work the same way as Navigator's. Or you can click the HISTORY button on the tool bar (at the left side of the window) and Explorer will display a list of all the sites you accessed to get to where you are now. To go to any of them, click the relevant name in the history listing.

* To get the program to routinely access a start page other than Microsoft's, go to the page you want, select Internet Options from the View menu, then click the General tab in the Options dialog box. Now click the Use Current button, then click 'OK'. Alternatively, type the URL of the page you want as a habitual start page into the dialog box's Address field.

BROWSER VOCABULARY

Navigator and Explorer differ mainly in superficial areas such as terminology, but you will find that you soon feel at home with the terminology your browser uses. In keeping with the Windows operating system, Explorer calls links 'shortcuts', home pages 'start pages', bookmarks 'favorites', and so on.

'get out the laptop, it's time to go home!'

PLUG-INS

* As new technologies are devised to increase the Web's abilities, more and more programs are needed to handle them.

plug-ins are popping up all over the place!

'did you know it can handle sound and video now?'

RIVAL ATTENTION

* Fortunately, rather than having to run these programs as a separate application, *browsers use the extra programs as plug-ins and helper software*. Developed by Netscape, plug-ins expand the range of a browser so that it can cope with STREAMING SOUND and VIDEO, prepared text documents, file-compression formats, and a multitude of other data formats.

* Inevitably, Microsoft has developed a rival system known as 'ActiveX controls' (though Internet Explorer can use plug-ins as well). ActiveX controls behave in much the same way as plug-ins and can also be integrated with the Windows operating system.

* ActiveX has yet to find great favour, partly because Netscape's plug-in system dominates cyberspace. Also, ActiveX programs are looked upon with suspicion by some because they are given free run of a computer system – if you download and install a rogue ActiveX control, the contents of your computer could possibly be trashed.

HELPMATE

✱ Another method for handling unknown data formats is to enable a browser to use 'helper' applications. Unlike plug-ins, helpers are stand-alone applications that your browser can call upon when it comes across a Web element it doesn't understand. For example, Adobe's Acrobat Reader is a stand-alone application that

you may be being watched and monitored as you surf

I'll give you two!

Active X hasn't found much favour

can be used as a helper when your browser locates a file in the popular Adobe PDF file format.

TAKING THE BISCUIT

✱ *Though surfing the Web might appear to be an essentially anonymous activity, in fact many sites are monitoring your activities*, noting when you last visited them, how long you stayed there, and any settings affected while you were visiting. To accomplish this, Web sites store small information files on your computer known as 'COOKIES'.

When the cookie crumbles

The use of cookies is not as sinister as it sounds. It's often useful to be able to visit sites – for example, news archives and search engines – that have been tailored to your personal requirements. In addition, sites that would otherwise ask you for a log-on name and password store them in a cookie to save you time and effort. Cookies are restricted to a maximum size of 4K and are time-sensitive. They should be removed from your computer once their expiry date is reached. Both Explorer and Navigator enable you to switch off the cookies system and reject the requests from servers. However, if you switch it off, you may not get access to some services you want.

LIFE IN THE FAST LANE

it's not all that fast online

* Get online and the first thing you'll notice is how slow it all is! Web pages download to your screen with often agonizing pauses, graphics build line by line, streaming sound and video take an age to download sufficiently to begin playing... In fact, the whole experience can be severely off-putting for Net novices.

KEY WORDS

NEWS FEED: the source of a Usenet connection such as your ISP

mirror sites can save time and money

Mirror, mirror

Mirror sites are copies of popular Web and FTP sites stored at locations in other countries. They offer speedy access to popular or geographically remote sites.

SLOW COACH

* And it's not just the Web. File transfers that begin promisingly at a rate of several kilobytes a second sometimes slow to just a few tens of bytes – and after an hour or more of watching a file dribble into your hard drive, while your phone bill mounts second by second, it's tempting to disconnect and abandon the transfer as a bad idea.

* *There are several solutions*. Choose an ISP that offers maximum modem speeds (currently 56K). Pick your time online carefully. Try to access the Net when the United States is sleeping (remembering that there are several US time zones).

* Ensure that any disk caching available from your browser is set to maximum, so time isn't wasted in needlessly downloading items from sites that you've accessed recently. Try always to make use of mirror sites that are geographically close

you can
wait
hours to
download
files...

To serve them all my days...

Somewhere between the World Wide Web and the browser software running on your computer will be the service that brings the one to the other, the Internet Service Provider (ISP). ISPs are companies that have one or more networks connected directly to the Internet and which, either for a fee or, increasingly, free of charge, allow you to connect your computer to their network over a telephone line and thereby to the Net. Until recently, a typical ISP would charge a monthly subscription in exchange for hard disk space on one of its computers and one or more email addresses (e.g. jerry.glenwright @serviceprovider.co.uk). In addition, ISPs usually provide a news feed from Usenet, so that you can also access the many thousands of newsgroups available (see pages 52-53).

to you – a popular American FTP site, for example, might well be mirrored in Europe.

✳ Netscape Navigator and Internet Explorer both offer a handy speed increase when you switch off AUTOMATIC IMAGE LOADING. Then, when a page is downloaded its graphics are replaced by an icon. To see the picture, all you have to do is right-click the icon.

POINT COUNTERPOINT

✳ ISP networks are connected directly to the Internet using the standard TCP/IP protocol. Your connection to the ISP's network, on the other hand, uses one of two protocols specially developed for the job: either PPP or SLIP. The latter was the first to be devised and was used extensively until the introduction of the far better PPP. Which to use is an issue decided by your ISP, and need not worry you.

CONNECTING TO THE NET

* An exponential increase in the number of ISPs followed the exponential rise in public interest in the Internet, and many have now faded from view. However, there are still plenty to choose from. Some charge a flat fee for unlimited access to the Net, while others offer a limited amount of time for a fee and charge extra if you spend more time online. A recent trend is to offer free access to private users, though this type of connection tends to be slightly 'cut-down'. Further details and a guide to what to look for when choosing an ISP are to be found in Chapter 6.

it's good to talk

VALUE-ADDED SERVICES

* As well as straightforward ISPs, there are a number of 'VALUE-ADDED' online services that offer a proprietary network for users to explore, plus a gateway to the Net.

* Before widespread public access to the

KEY WORDS

PPP:
Point-to-Point Protocol, used by ISPs to connect customers' computers to the Internet via telephone lines

SLIP:
Serial Line Internet Protocol – similar to PPP, but not quite as efficient

people demanded information about the internet

we want to know

tell us more

help me please

Internet, those who wanted to explore online computing offered or accessed bulletin boards services (see pages 50-51). BBS software was available for many personal computers from different manufacturers – but once up and running, any other personal computer, even one that is ostensibly incompatible, can dial into the board and make use of what's to be found there.

on-line games were very popular in the 1980s

✱ The BBS scene enjoyed massive popularity during the 1980s – especially in America where telephone calls were cheaper. Some BBSs became immensely popular and expanded the original theme to provide multiple telephone lines with several networked boards.

✱ This enabled a number of users to dial in simultaneously, and multiple-access BBSs began to offer ONLINE GAMES and REAL-TIME CHAT. Their popularity prompted several of the largest to charge for access, and from this grew commercial online services such as CompuServe, Delphi, Prodigy and America Online (AOL).

Attractions online

The rise of the Internet resulted in the demise of many online services, but others interpreted the future correctly, adapted their service to include an Internet gateway and became value-added services. Several are still available, though an awkward pricing structure and active censoring lead many to avoid them. Perhaps the two best known ones are AOL and CompuServe (now no longer under separate ownership, since AOL bought CompuServe). Both offer Internet access and a great deal of online help, as well as a range of services such as shopping, chat, games, listings and so on – though much of this stuff can be had for free directly from the Net itself.

real-time chat became a common thing

SEX ON THE NET

✱ Wherever there are concentrations of people, some will want to look at pictures of others undraped. This, whatever we may think of it, is arguably a natural human impulse. It is also one that's catered for in gargantuan proportions on the Internet.

Hard core?

One problem with porn on the net is that virtually every other country in the world has attitudes to sex that many Britons would consider lax. Whereas in the UK the term 'soft-core' normally refers to the sort of pictures available in tabloid newspapers, elsewhere (including the US, all of our European neighbours and much of Latin America) soft-core is considered to be something graphically different.

there is plenty of nasty
stuff to see - but you
don't have to look

soft porn doesn't
shock me ?

different countries
have different
attitudes to sex

NOT FOR THE SQUEAMISH...

✱ A dearth of effective CENSORSHIP — unless you're using a value-added service — means that the Web is positively awash with sites devoted to providing pornography in all its guises. In addition, Usenet has hundreds of newsgroups devoted to the subject of SEX, some featuring discussions of activities you either didn't know existed,

not there

previously assumed impossible, or avoided for reasons of good taste or fear of the law.

* *Fortunately for the prudish (and squeamish), all of the Usenet sex newsgroups and picture posts are easily avoided*. After all, you don't have to subscribe to them, or read their contents or download their pictures. Those who admire the male and female form, however, especially aficionados interested in watching it contort itself into positions physiotherapists might advise against, can log in to Usenet and have a field day.

parents need to monitor their children's surfing

PORNOGRAPHY AND THE WEB

* The Web, on the other hand, is a little trickier. True, commercial sex sites almost invariably have a 'front door' that warns of what's beyond and requires an explicit click to enter, generally after sternly regaling you with a lot of pseudo-legal stuff. But the front door itself usually sports one or two TITILLATING

DON'T subscribe and DON'T read the contents

commercial sex sites usually give a warning

pictures, intended to WHET THE APPETITE and draw in potential customers.

89

okay, that's got
rid of nanny

SEARCH AND ENJOY

* Because it is such a vast place, it can be difficult to find things on the Web (pornography excepted!). There's just so much out there in cyberspace that to traverse it all in search of a particular item of information, picture, sound, or what have you, would take perhaps years. That's why search engines such as AltaVista, and other methods of cataloguing and indexing, have evolved. Essentially, they all maintain indexes of key words regularly culled from the Web.

little boys will
always find something
to snigger about

'well, without sex
there'd be no
shopping!'

KEY WORDS

BOOLEAN:
a form of algebra, devised by Scottish mathematician George Boole in the 19th century, based on notions of logic

ALTAVISTA IN ACTION

* Using AltaVista is a simple matter of pointing your browser at its Web site then entering one or more key words or phrases into the text area provided. Click the '<u>SEARCH</u>' button or press the enter/return key, and AltaVista checks its index and presents you with all the pages featuring your key word or phrase that it has succeeded in finding. This could be as few as one or as many as a million, depending on what it is you're looking for. The results are <u>RANKED</u> in order of best match, and each has a link that you can click in order to go straight to the site.

REFINING SEARCH OPTIONS

* *It's possible to initiate highly sophisticated searching with AltaVista* using BOOLEAN OPERATORS such as 'and', 'or' and 'not'. For the uninitiated, the results can be spectacularly unexpected. What's more, it's easy to waste hours by embarking on an orgy of surfing, tempted by the results of an AltaVista search. It's much like getting side-tracked when you're scouring a dictionary for a particular word ('Good grief! I didn't know "spintry" meant that!').

clever searching is a must online

* Try to narrow down a search by using specific phrases or key words – search for '+Marx +Bros+Duck +Soup', rather than say, 'Marx Brothers films'. Pedantry and a certain amount of lateral thinking are what CLEVER SEARCHING is all about, otherwise you'll end up wading through masses of text before finding what it is you actually want.

nanny always knows best

NANNYWARE

A possible solution to the problem of restricting children's Net access is to install one of the so-called 'nanny' software packages on your computer. These are intended to filter out sites that have a sexual content or theme. However, the software may differ from you in what it considers unacceptable, so these packages are not a complete solution. What's more, children at the dawn of the 21st century almost invariably know more about software than their parents do – so you may find that your kids can circumnavigate the nanny software with ease. Probably the most effective solution is simply to be on-hand when they're online.

it's all gone
horribly wrong

WHEN THINGS GO WRONG

* Usually surfing the Web is a straightforward affair, involving nothing more complicated than pointing to a link and clicking it — but every so often a Web browser will return error messages after failing to access a particular site. These errors take many forms and occur for a variety of reasons. Some are cyberspace dead-ends, others typing errors but many can be worked around.

try not to get stuck
in a cyberspace jam

'FILE NOT FOUND'

* *Perhaps the most common error message you'll encounter* tersely announces '404 file not found'.

* Though initially impressive, this error message simply means the page specified by the URL that your browser is trying to resolve can't be located. The reason for this may be that the page doesn't exist any more (a day is a long time in cyberspace, and Web sites change continuously).

* Or it might mean that there's a typo in the URL. Given the complexity of some Web addresses, this is a likely

AUTHOR ERROR

Sometimes a site's own author misspells a link. In which case, by slightly altering any obviously 'weird' bits you may eventually be able to reach it.

'you will learn
to spell,
you horrible
lot'

possibility – especially if you've typed the URL into the browser's Location field, rather than following a link. You only have to type a full stop, dash, hyphen or oblique in the wrong place, and the browser goes off to never-never land.

TRY, TRY AND TRY AGAIN

✳ Sometimes the site specified in a URL is still active but the HTML document isn't. For example, let's say you've clicked a link with an embedded URL that points to:

http://www.wimpleware.co.uk/books/internet.html

All is spelled and punctuated correctly, but the browser returns the dreaded <u>404</u> error message. Try this. Click in the browser's Address field and backspace over (i.e. delete) the internet.html part of the URL, so that you have:

http://www.wimpleware.co.uk/books/

Now press enter/return. The browser will try again. If it now displays a Web page, the reason for the previous failure was that the subpage internet.html of the Web site **www.wimpleware.co.uk** is no longer available. It may have been changed and renamed, or else removed. You can 'step back' up the URL, deleting parts of the address, until either you reach a valid Web page or it becomes obvious that no such site exists.

As if by magic...

Another common error message is 'The server does not have a DNS entry'. This is more irksome than the 404 message since you can't get around it easily. It means that the DNS server was unable to resolve the URL into a numerical address, the inference being that the site does not exist. Once again, check the spelling and punctuation – making sure your typing of uppercase/lowercase is correct, since URLs are case-sensitive. Also, it's worth trying again with the same address. Occasionally, for no obvious reason, things that have gone wrong go right again seconds later.

sometimes things right themselves for no real reason

ALL FROM THE WEB

NO
go away

* The popularity of the World Wide Web has effectively transformed it into a one-stop market of Net services. As well as surfing Web sites, you can traverse Gopherspace and download files from FTP servers from a standard browser without the need for plug-ins or separate clients. In addition, the Web can serve in place of the Net's two other most important services,

you can be refused access to some popular sites

Usenet and email. Both are available from Web sites that can be accessed with an ordinary browser.

More the merrier

DejaNews offers much more than a web-based newsfeed. You can check the posting history of the author of any message, discover which newsgroups he or she has posted to in the past, and read his or her past postings. And conversely, of course, others can familiarize themselves with your posting history!

NEWS BEAT

* *The DejaNews Web site provides an archive of every newsgroup available from Usenet* that is continuously updated. Using DejaNews, you can post and read messages just as if you were using a news client to access Usenet.

* You can subscribe to as many newsgroups as you choose and, if you want to, have each day's messages from your chosen groups concatenated into a single file and then transmitted to you by EMAIL.

* **DejaNews keeps archives of many more newsgroups than are available from a typical ISP news feed**. ISPs tend to offer access to the more popular ones only; also, it's possible to miss lots of messages on particularly active groups if your ISP doesn't provide sufficiently frequent updates. DejaNews solves both problems, by providing an ARCHIVE of Usenet in its entirety and enabling you to search back over several years of postings.

you can search back through years of posting history

'and now for the deja news'

REGISTER AND BE DAMNED!

* Although you can access the DejaNews site on a casual basis, you can also register and tailor the service to your exact requirements. This service is called MYDEJANEWS.

* If you register with DejaNews, you will be assigned a mailbox (with a name of your choice), which can be extremely useful if you subscribe to mailing lists or want to filter out the kind of junk mail that can clutter up an ISP-provided mailbox.

ENTRY DENIED

With millions of pages and billions of bytes of data travelling to and fro through cyberspace, it's no wonder that some Web site servers get so bogged down that they're unable to respond to any more 'callers'. If your attempt to access a Web page fails because the server is too busy, you'll be regaled with a message indicating that your connection with server xyz has been refused. The solution is simple: try again immediately (several times), and if you still don't get connected wait a while and try again later. You may find that some sites, such as university departments, are offline to outsiders at certain times of the day or at the weekend.

EMAIL VIA THE WEB

* Several Web-based email services are available. One of the first was Hotmail, and it is certainly one of the best known. Anyone can acquire a Hotmail mailbox. And you can choose any name you like for your email address: the name of a company or organization, an alter ego, anything. All you have to do is to complete an online questionnaire, but there's nothing very daunting about it and most of the questions are mundane.

hotmail was one of the first web based email services

POP3 AND SMTP

Email uses two simple and universal protocols to send and receive communications and these are called SMTP (Simple Mail Transfer Protocol) and POP3 (Post Office Protocol) respectively.

WEB MAILBOXES

* These WEB MAILBOXES work in exactly the same as an ordinary POP3 mailbox. In fact, the only difference is that they have a Web-based front-end with which to access them.

* As with other email services, *you can send messages accompanied by file attachments*, and organize and catalogue your mail in any way you want. They make convenient filters for those who subscribe to mailing lists and the like, since the output can be sent to separate Web mailboxes.

* Web-based email services (like those provided by many ISPs) enable you to set up mailboxes for your company, club or other organization easily and entirely for free. By using several mailboxes, you can give yourself ALTERNATIVE IDENTITIES.

PUTTING UP A PAGE

darling
it's so big

* Eventually, after spending many hours traversing the Web's tangled avenues, you may feel the urge to PUBLISH a Web page of your own.

accommodation on hard-drives is made available by ISPs for customers' use

I'll take **204** please

you can have as many electronic mailboxes as you like

SPACIOUS ACCOMMODATION

Most ISPs make an amount of hard-drive space available to their customers – typically around 20MB, which is more than enough to store the HTML code and files necessary to publish a good-looking Web page. You may be motivated to create a site featuring sounds and graphics, perhaps plus files to download; or content with a more straightforward site, consisting of a page or two of text, a family picture and a few links to some of your favourite sites. Either way, creating the site will be an enjoyable experience, and you'll weave a tiny part of yourself into the fabric of cyberspace.

* *Putting up a page is a relatively easy task* (especially if you use an HTML editor software package) and, best of all, you don't require anyone's PERMISSION or approval. If you've always wanted to publish what you consider to be your masterwork you can do so without having to trawl round publishers in search of someone willing to take it on.

no need to worry about rejection, you can remain anonymous

97

A PAGE OF YOUR OWN

✱ By publishing online, you'll probably reach an audience far wider than that enjoyed by a printed work. And unlike vanity publishing, when you pay to have your work printed yourself, it won't cost you anything on top of what you're already paying for a connection to the Net.

you don't want to borrow

more sugar!

'but we all borrow freely on the net'

Copyright?

Although copyright is just as applicable to something published electronically as it is to traditional forms of publication, on the Web attitudes tend to be more relaxed. Most Webmasters won't mind a bit if you pinch their background wallpaper or an image or two and use them on your own page.

ALL YOUR OWN WORK

✱ Lots of authors have published their works on the Internet. Some are of remarkably HIGH QUALITY and some have proved enormously popular – though of course there are plenty of strident diatribes and other dire outpourings available on the Net, as well!

CREATING A WEB PAGE

✱ Constructing a Web page doesn't have to involve learning complicated programming languages or wielding paint packages to create snazzy images. Some of the more SUCCESSFUL sites are off-the-wall efforts created by ordinary people who have an interest in the quirky and unusual or a hobby that provides inspiration or imagery for a lively Web page.

you don't need a lot of gadgets to make a good home page

come on in
and visit

people from all around the world
will soon start to visit you on
your home page

HTML EDITORS

✱ There are plenty of free and shareware HTML editors available from FTP servers. These make the process of creating a Web page very easy.

✱ Using an editor, you simply position the elements you want to publish (text, images, buttons, bullets, and so on) on a page and the software 'writes' the HTML code. The final step is to upload the HTML code and the elements you've used on the page to the hard-drive space at your ISP account.

✱ You'll then need to PUBLICIZE the new page. Because there is widespread access to the Net, news of a good new page travels fast. Create an interesting page, and you might have thousands of people a day from all around the world paying it a visit!

unusual hobbies are the ideal thing to put on your home page

GETTING THERE FROM HOME

Storing all your favourite sites as embedded links on your own home page is a handy way to navigate the Web. You can set your browser to access your home page on start-up, then click the links of the pages you want to visit from the convenient list.

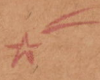

CHAPTER 3

THE INS AND OUTS OF EMAIL

* Email is easy to use, informal and almost instantaneous, whether you're sending a message to someone in the same town or on the other side of the world. Unlike a telephone call (where you speak voice to voice, ear to ear, with the other person and suffer the inevitable inhibitions which that brings), email enables you to create a quick, cheery message, send it in real time (almost), and say what you want more or less without inhibition.

hi mum, just a quick note to say...

email is quick, easy to use and informal

MAIL ROUTES

* Answering email is even easier. All you have to do is click on the 'REPLY' button offered by most email software, type, and then click the 'SEND' button. Your mail promptly wings its way to the recipient, often in less time than it takes you to close your email program.

* *Email does not come to you directly.* Messages travel between the mail servers of host computers and, as a private Net user, you have to log on to your ISP's mail server to collect your mail (unless

POP GROUP

Don't confuse the POP3 (Post Office Protocol, version 3) mail protocol with the other kind of POP that figures in Net terminology. POP (without the 3) is the acronym for Points Of Presence, an ISP's local dial-in points.

@ *

\#

you're attached to an office Intranet where mail is sent directly to your machine). *After you've collected your email, it's usually deleted from the ISP's mail server*.

✳ Similarly, when you send an email, it travels from your computer to your ISP's mail server and from there it is routed out over the Internet, possibly via many host computers, until it eventually reaches its destination.

sorry mate, this one's got to go round the block first

email isn't sent directly

✳ Although this indirect method adds to the time it takes for messages to be delivered, it circumvents the need for you to be online in order to receive them. Instead, emails are stored on the server until you download them.

EMAIL-ONLY SERVICES

All ISPs offer email as part of their range of services, in addition to access to the Web and Usenet. However, it's possible to side-step the other services if you don't need or want them and just have an email account, usually at a considerable financial saving. Some ISPs offer free email-only accounts via special dial-up nodes, though you do still have to pay for use of the telephone and perhaps put up with advertising. These ISPs make money in two ways: by splitting the revenue generated by use of the telephone line with the phone companies and by selling advertising space. Paradoxically, an email-only account doesn't limit you to email only. You can access Archie and FTP servers, albeit in a rather roundabout way, and even have Web pages sent to your mailbox.

MORE ABOUT EMAIL

* Like Web URLs, email addresses are used as an exact pointer to a destination at a host computer on the Net. Every bit of the address – including its spelling and punctuation – must be exactly right, or the email will not reach its destination.

emails get bounced back
if the address is wrong

THERE ON FILE

* If you address an email incorrectly, either as a result of mistyping or because you've been given an address that's invalid, then your ISP's mail server will make the fact known to you soon enough. When you send an email, its address is checked by the mail server – then if it's recognized as being valid, it is routed across the Net immediately. Emails that don't pass muster at the mail server are 'BOUNCED' back to the sender along with a brief message outlining the problem.

HISTORY IN THE MAKING

* *Emails can provide a ready-made history of past communications.* Those you receive are stored on your computer until you choose to delete them. Conversely, those you send are stored as back-ups on your machine until you delete them, usually in a 'Sent' directory that you can examine at any time.

* Automatic back-ups mean that it's easy to browse backwards and forwards

I'd like a record of
everything, please

through your emails, much as you'd browse through a pocket diary, noting people you haven't contacted for a while, remembering things you ought to have done, dates, places, and so on.

* There is, however, one small drawback to everything being on file. Other people have a record of your postings. Respond to an email in the heat of the moment and you might wish you hadn't: the recipient may retain a copy of your outburst on his or her machine.

you can look up everything you've ever sent and check times, addresses and so on

MULTIPLICITY

* It's as easy to send many copies of the same email as it is to send one. All mailer software offers a 'Cc' field into which you can plug a list of email addresses from an online address book (most mailer packages provide one). Click 'Send', and the message is sent to everyone on the list. However, this is not always considered good

it's not good netiquette

it is not good practice to send unnecessary emails

netiquette – some people routinely forward emails to tens, or sometimes even hundreds, of others unnecessarily, wasting BANDWIDTH as well as the recipients' time.

WHERE YOU'RE AT . . .

All email addresses include @ (see pages 32-33) and use the Domain Name System (see pages 38-39). For example,

jerry@wimpleware.co.uk

equates to user Jerry, located at the host domain wimpleware, a company, based in the UK.

I'm glad I looked you up after all this time

but which format?

don't worry about
file formats

Which format?

Uuencode/decode is a Unix-to-Unix encoding and decoding algorithm devised to enable file-copying between Unix hosts. It is widely used. MIME (Multi-purpose Internet Mail Extension) is an encoding format created by Microsoft, and one that is becoming increasingly accepted on the Net. BinHex is an Apple Macintosh format that has been around for a considerable time and which continues to be used.

TRANSLATION

Two processes occur to make attachments acceptable to email protocols. They're translated into one of several file formats that transform their binary code into what looks like plain ASCII text; and files larger than 64K are broken into 64K blocks.

EMAIL ATTACHMENTS

* As well as sending plain ASCII text in an email, you can attach all manner of files - images, programs, data files from spread-sheets, word-processor documents and the like - to it.

REATTACHMENT

* **At the receiving end, the attachment is stripped from the email** and then either used as a stand-alone program or imported into a suitable application, such as a spreadsheet or word-processor program. Often – for example, when accessing images – you can simply click on the attachment and have the computer run a suitable application to display it.

send these
please

you can send any
manner of
attachments with
your emails

FILE FORMATS

* Depending on your email client, you'll use one of three translation formats for sending attachments: Uuencode/decode, MIME, or BinHex.

* *In practice, encoding, decoding and reassembly will, for the most part, occur without your knowledge or intervention.* You'll simply send emails with attachments, and receive others with appended files ready for use.

MIMEs have the word MIME in their top line

FORMING AN ATTACHMENT

* Emails are restricted to a maximum size of 64K of plain ASCII text. Clearly that isn't nearly enough to send even an average-sized colour image, which might well occupy half a megabyte or more. Practically all programs (other than perhaps the tiniest utility) will amount to considerably more than 64K; and neither graphics nor computer programs take the form of plain-text files. A process of TRANSLATION must occur before a file is emailed.

MIME ARTIST

Occasionally the encoded file appears to be embedded in the email, following the message text. A uuencoded part of an email message can be easily recognized because it always starts with the word 'Begin...', followed by nonsense text. MIMEs have the word MIME... in their top line. Either file type can be retrieved by selecting its text and cutting it from the parent email, then pasting it into a word-processor document and saving it as a text file. A suitable utility, such as StuffIt, can then be used to translate it back into its binary form.

'let's form an attachment'

COMPRESSING FILES

* As well as being encoded, large files are often compressed using any one of a number of popular compression programs. These strip redundant code from files, making them smaller and so quicker (and cheaper) to send via email. Files compressed in this way must be decompressed by the user at the receiving end - a simple task using one of the many freeware decompression programs.

EASY CRUNCH

you can decompress files to send...

STUFF AND NONSENSE

StuffIt is an extremely versatile utility: as well as providing comprehensive file compression and encoding options, it can make sense of numerous weird file formats generated by other compression programs found on the Net.

it's stuff and nonsense

* *On Windows machines the Zip utility is perhaps the most popular compression program*. This is available in two flavours: as a command line-driven DOS utility and as a fully-blown Windows application. Both are competent and easy to use. StuffIt is Zip's counterpart on the Apple Macintosh computer. Unix machines use TAR, among others. Utilities that handle all these formats, sometimes from within a single program, can be had from FTP servers.

QUOTE...UNQUOTE

❋ Email communications have engendered their own ways of doing things. It's common to see parts of a message or even the whole message QUOTED in a reply. Sometimes quotes will appear as a block of text at the beginning of an email; or they may be broken into brief sentences, just one or two lines long, with the sender's answers written between them.

I quote

quoting helps to keep things informal

❋ *Quoting helps to keep an air of informality* and enables writers to be brief in a way that wouldn't be permissible in a

...and they can be pumped up again at the other side of the globe

normal letter, while still providing a perfectly acceptable reply. These quotes are useful for the recipient, too, as a memory aid – send a lot of email and it's easy to forget what it was you sent or who you sent it to.

Restrain yourself

Netiquette suggests that you should restrain the quoting habit when responding to email from list servers. It takes just two or three correspondents quoting an original message plus subsequent ones and an email can grow to outrageous proportions, wasting a considerable amount of bandwidth. And you can imagine what the average Net geek makes of receiving an email which wastes bandwidth...

SMILEYS AND OTHER GIZMOS

* Another weird form of communicating that has arisen uniquely in the world of electronic post is the smiley. It looks like :-) or sometimes :) and, as a user of the Net, it will be all but impossible to avoid coming into contact with the little smiling face. Smileys are used to soften blows, convey irony, or fill an otherwise embarrassing gap.

wear your heart on your sleeve with emoticons

Hi   go away

EMOTIONAL SHORTHAND

* Worse (or better, if you're someone who likes them), smileys are just one tiny member of a whole family of what are called 'EMOTICONS' – icons embedded in otherwise plain text that are intended to convey an emotion.

* The best advice is to use emoticons sparingly. The Net is split roughly 70/30 between those who love them (or, at least,

EMOTICONS			
:->	Sarcastic	(_|_)	Mooning
8-)	Sunglasses	}:>	Fiendish
;-)	Winking	:-p	Tongue out
:-o	Oh!	:D	Big grin
0:-)	Angelic	:-X	Saying nothing

use them regularly) and those who'd rather introduce their private parts to a shoe box full of scorpions than ever see one again.

* *Whichever camp you fall into, have respect for the other*. At worst, smileys are irritating. At best, they're a simple way to convey a bit of cheer in what can otherwise be a rather cold medium.

THE ARGOT OF THE NET

read LOL and your correspondent is laughing out loud

* Wearing your heart on your sleeve emailwise doesn't stop at emoticons. There's a veritable lexicon of acronyms and abbreviations bandied about by almost every Net user – even people who ordinarily would shudder at hip slang.

* Actually, *acronyms and abbreviations can be a useful way to speed email replies* and keep bandwidth usage to a minimum. However, hip kids, US college professors and the like often make use of the most complex acronyms, which rather defeats the aim and keeps newbies at the cold outer fringes of the Netiverse.

* Some abbreviations are borrowings from the real world, such as RTFM (Read The ******* Manual) and SNAFU (Situation Normal, All ****** Up). Others can be entirely blamed on Net users: BTW (By The Way), FYI (For Your Information), LOL (Laughing Out Loud), and so on.

LOADS OF E-JUNK

If you think the pile of junk mail thudding onto your doormat is annoying, just wait till you get started with email! At first e-junk is sparse, but become an active Net user and soon enough your mailbox will be swamped with unsolicited email. Most plentiful among the offending items are get-rich-quick schemes, invitations to exotic personal encounters, pleas from incapacitated children, and an apparent army of itinerant cheerleaders who want to sell you their underwear.

groan

if you think junk mail is bad brace yourself for e-junk

I wish I could find my diary

EMAIL SOFTWARE

* To use email, you need a mailer (email application) on your computer. If you have a PC running Windows 95 or 98, you already have suitable software. Windows 95 comes with Microsoft Mail; and Windows 98 is shipped with Outlook Express, a combined news and email program with many other features, including an address book and an appointments calendar.

email applications come complete with built-in address books

swalk

U.S. MAIL

there are many popular mailers available

MAILERS GALORE

* Popular Web browsers such as Netscape Navigator come with mail software. And there are many freeware and shareware mailers from third parties that you can install and use alongside your other Net tools.

* Probably the most popular third-party email application on the Mac is EUDORA, a comprehensive mailer that handles multiple email identities with ease and offers mail filtering, back-ups and other useful features.

* Best of all, Eudora is a free download in its 'Light' version. Or you can plump for the all-singing Eudora Pro and pay a shareware fee. Eudora is also a popular PC application; so is Pegasus, another independent email application.

SESSION TIME

* A typical session with a mailer will go something like this. You start up the mailer, which will in turn initiate a connection to your ISP. If you have email waiting to be sent, the mailer will log on to the ISP mail server and send your emails for you. The software will then check for incoming mail and, if you have any, download it to your computer. You'll then be <u>NOTIFIED</u> that there's unread mail.

you'll wonder how you managed without email

you have
new mail

your mailer will tell you when there's new mail

* *Typically, logging on for email in this way will be your first task during a session online.* Once your email has been safely downloaded and read, you can leave the mailer running in the background while you use a browser or some other Net tool, so that it can periodically (and automatically) log on to the mail server and check for incoming mail.

OVERSPECIFIED?

When choosing a mailer, pause to consider whether you need all the (undoubtedly useful) bells and whistles offered by some of the more comprehensive mailers. Although great for the experienced, they can make mailer software needlessly complex for novices.

Workalikes

Mail programs all work in much the same way. Which one you opt for is likely to depend on factors such as what came free with your computer or from your ISP, or perhaps what you use at work and are therefore familiar with.

111

SENDING AN EMAIL

* Sending an email need not involve anything more complicated than clicking a 'Compose' or 'New message' button, specifying an address (or selecting one from your mailer's

gone are the days when keeping in touch was a chore

address book) and typing your message, then clicking the 'Send' button. If you want to send a file along with the email, there's usually an 'Attachments' button of some kind.

More repeats!

Most mailers quote the original message in its entirety in the reply window. You can trim this to suit, cut it completely, or use a mailer preferences dialog to switch this feature off.

SENDING A REPLY

* *Replying to email is equally easy*. When your software downloads emails it will present them in a window, usually alongside a closed envelope or some other device denoting that you haven't yet read them. To read an email, you simply click on the relevant item in this window.

* Replying requires nothing more than clicking a REPLY button, usually located somewhere in the same window that displays the emails. There's no need to enter an address when replying, because the mailer software will take the address from the original message. Simply type your reply, quoting from the original if you wish and click the Send button.

email is so
easy to use

just signing off now

some would-be artists make up complex
signatures from ASCII characters

SIGNING OFF

✱ If instructed to do so, your mailer will automatically tack a 'SIGNATURE FILE' onto the end of your emails, performing a similar task to headed writing paper. This is a pre-prepared text file containing, say, your name and address or telephone number.

✱ Many people like to include a humorous quote or witticism in their signature file (and, just occasionally, they're actually amusing). Others indulge in an orgy of what's called 'ASCII art' – an email version of a spray-painted signature, created from ASCII characters.

Unknown artists

Some ASCII artists fashion extremely complex and clever drawings, cartoons or variations on the letters of their names. Sadly, most remain unviewed by recipients, who rarely bother to scroll to the end of a message in order to see the signature or the art.

snazzy signatures
can very often
go unnoticed

Arghhh!

Like smileys, signature files serve a purpose – but it's a limited one, and probably the majority of recipients either ignore them or are irritated by them. Use with discretion!

please, no
more silly
signatures

113

OTHER USES OF EMAIL

vrooom

rat a tat a tat

* Email can be put to a variety of uses in addition to the more obvious ones. For example, you can join an email discussion group, or 'mailing list'. A mailing list is similar to a Usenet newsgroup in that a group of like-minded people

share unusual hobbies using ordinary household email

come together to exchange information and views on a specific topic, or to rant and rave about it.

We like lists

If you have an unusual hobby, a mailing list is a great way to meet people with a similar interest, swap news and views with them, and ask for or give help. Like newsgroups, mailing lists tend to be unmoderated and often feature some pretty off-the-wall characters only too willing to vent their spleen by tearing you off a strip!

ASK ARCHIE

* *Email is also an excellent way to locate files without having to interrogate an Archie server interactively*. Accessing Archie servers in this way isn't quick – but it does free your machine for other uses, and it widens the scope for users who have email-only Net accounts.

* To email an Archie server, type 'archie@' and the address of a local Archie server in your mailer's 'To' field. Type a space in the 'Subject' field if your mailer insists on a subject being specified; otherwise, leave this field blank. Make the first line of the message 'SEND MAILTO' followed by your email address. On the second and

subsequent lines, type the commands you want the Archie server to perform, such as 'find StuffIt'. Use only one command on each line and put the command 'quit' on the final line. Send the email, and you should have a reply within a few hours.

there must be a better way

mailing lists forward
messages to subscribers

MAILING LISTS

* Unlike a newsgroup (which is a 'central' collection of messages accessed via a news server), a MAILING LIST forwards the messages it receives to its subscribers. The mailing list is managed automatically by a list server, which maintains a directory of subscribers and sends a copy of postings to everyone on the list.

* The only human intervention occurs if a mailing list is MODERATED – that is, when junk postings are weeded out by a human operator.

Educating Archie

One problem with emailing Archie is that it's difficult to narrow the search – so be prepared to receive a tidal wave of information. It's worth sending an email to Archie saying 'send mailto youremailaddress' on the first line and 'help' on the next. In return, you'll receive a list of all the commands Archie understands, plus tips on how to make searches more specific.

Unsubscribing

Before you subscribe to a mailing list, make sure you know how to unsubscribe. Receiving hundreds of dull or off-topic messages soon palls. Unsubscribing is similar to subscribing – you simply send a message to the list server containing a line such as 'unsubscribe atari8' or 'signoff atari8'.

we'd like to unsubscribe

unsubscribing is easy

MASTERS OF DISGUISE

* While some email correspondents make sure you won't forget who they are (by using complex ASCII-art signatures and the like), others go to even greater lengths to cover their electronic tracks and prevent you discovering their identity.

Paranoid – me?

Though practical jokers, criminals and the clinically insane do indeed bend email to their shady purposes, the majority of messages you'll receive will be perfectly straightforward communications from friends and colleagues, laced with only a very small amount of spam, fake virus warnings and the occasional chain letter – you can use email with impunity.

USURPING AN ADDRESS

it's easy to forge
email addresses

* *Forging an email address is a simple act*. Your email address is automatically included with every email you send – but all you have to do to disguise the originating address is type a fake one into the Preferences/Options dialog box of your mailer software.

* Use an address that doesn't exist and the recipient will find out about it as soon as he or she tries to respond to your message – since the reply will be bounced back from the mail server. But if you enter an email address from an account that exists (for instance, one from a World Wide Web-based mail service or that of an unsuspecting third party), then the recipient may never know.

* All of which means that if you receive a strange email from a normally sane friend, don't automatically assume that he or she

has gone off the rails, is inebriated, or suddenly and unjustifiably hates you! It might simply be that a prankster has sent you an email using your friend's address.

TRACING THE SENDER

* There are other ways to remain anonymous when sending emails. Web-based REMAILERS forward anonymous emails and handle replies.

tee, hee

giggle

email is often used by practical jokers

* To use a remail service you register with it online – which provides a degree of anonymity because the remailer removes the giveaway header information from your emails.

* However, those who remain anonymous for nefarious purposes can be tracked down by law-enforcement agencies, who will insist that the remailer provides them with the OFFENDER'S DETAILS.

you can easily find out who is playing email pranks

Dodgy dealings

If you suspect that you've been sent a 'dodgy' email, view its 'properties' and check out where it originated. You'll be able to determine the name of the sending server and other useful clues, and find out whether the message has been forwarded by a remailer.

emailers who remain anonymous for dodgy purposes can be challenged in law

117

WEB-BASED MAIL

* The easiest way to adopt a persona (whether grata or non grata) is to register with a Web-based mail service such as Hotmail or use the facilities provided by DejaNews, Yahoo and others. Web email works just like 'real' POP3 email. You point your browser at the mail service's Web page, type your user name and password, and are then presented with the contents of your mail box. You can compose and send messages, append file attachments, and generally do anything you are able to do with 'ordinary' email.

DIRECTORY ENQUIRIES

You want to track down long-lost friends, former work colleagues or boy/girlfriends, or those who owe you money? The easiest way is to use Web-based email directories (see page 187 for URLs). These create catalogues of email addresses sourced in a number of ways, but principally culled from services such as Usenet and the Web's DejaNews that the addressees have visited.

MATTERS OF IDENTITY

* *Registration is a painless affair*, requiring answers to such innocuous questions as which country you're in and what your hobbies are. You have to put up

tonight I'm
Juan Kerr

you can adopt any persona you fancy and remain incognito

e-snooper

with a certain amount of advertising based on the profile you give during the registration process, but it's a small price to pay for unlimited email addresses tailored exactly to your needs. **✶ And, of course, you can use your new multiple email identities for good as well as evil!** Web email is a perfect way to subscribe to a mailing list, since you can use the Web-based mailbox to separate the hundreds of emails that a mailing list generates from other email, making it easier to manage both. You can also set up Web email addresses for your company, spouse or children.

PRIVACY ON PARADE

✶ Web mail offers a similar level of privacy to POP3/SMTP email. Under normal circumstances your mail is entirely secure and can be read only by you. However, almost any data winging its way across the Internet can be intercepted by the determined. A glitch in a server may transport your message to the email equivalent of a black hole. Or you might simply leave your machine unattended for a few minutes, giving the unscrupulous the opportunity to read your emails. In short, no mail is ENTIRELY SECURE.

SNOOPERS

One way to get an edge on e-snoopers and crank up the level of your security is to use encryption. Encrypting the contents of your email messages transforms otherwise plain text into total gobbledygook that is all but impossible to decipher – even using powerful computers and the talents of bribe-hungry maths postgraduates. So much so in fact, that some governments legislate against its use.

UNDER LOCK AND KEY

I'm totally paranoid

* Encryption is available in several forms, but most formats employ what's known as a 'key system'. The key is generated from a phrase, supplied by you, that is applied to the text using a sophisticated algorithm to scramble and unscramble it.

keep your secret key in a place that no-one else will look

BENDING THE RULES

Though strong encryption software such as PGP is prohibited for export outside America, the US imposes no equivalent ban on printed matter. To bend the rules, PGP was published as a book of source code, and this has since been typed and compiled back into a binary file. It's therefore relatively easy to acquire very strong encryption software virtually anywhere in the world (usually via the Web – try typing 'PGP' into a search engine such as AltaVista).

SECRET KEYS

* *The most effective key-system encryption is known as 'public-key cryptography'.* It uses two keys, a PUBLIC KEY which you give to anyone who wants it, and a PRIVATE KEY which you keep entirely secret. Once a correspondent has encrypted a message to you using the public key, it can then only be unscrambled using your private key.

* Public-key cryptography is so effective that the US government PROHIBITS the export of public-key encryption programs based on keys using more than 512 bits (known as 'strong cryptography'). The French and the Russian governments have banned public encryption entirely.

* Cryptographers recommend 768-bit keys for personal use, 1,024-bit keys for corporate use, and 2,048-bit keys for unimaginably valuable secrets – or the totally paranoid.

✱ There are many sources of encryption software, but PRETTY GOOD PRIVACY (PGP; see page 189 for URL) offers a freeware version featuring key encryption based on two well-known strong algorithms, RSA and Diffie-Hellman. PGP is considered highly secure if it's used properly.

SIMPLE SCRAMBLE

✱ One text-scrambling method you'll see all the time in emails and Usenet postings is known as ROT13. This uses a method of scrambling messages familiar to all children, that of substituting one letter of the alphabet for another – in this case for the 13th successive letter (so that A becomes N).

ROT13 is a popular encryption device

✱ Though simple, this device is enough to keep the inappropriate from unsuitable eyes – not revealing a film plot in a Usenet movie-fan newsgroup for example. Some mailers unscramble ROT13 messages on command, so you don't have to bother.

the American government wants to gain access to private keys

Stone the escrows!

In a bid to foil the privacy of its citizens (and consequently those of other countries), the US government devised a system of gaining access to keys – a process known as Government Access to Keys (GAK), popularly called 'key escrow'. This involves corporate and certain other users breaking up their private keys and lodging the pieces with several 'responsible' agencies sworn not to reveal them under all but abnormal circumstances. Companies willing to comply with these conditions are permitted to employ stronger keys than usual. The idea is that the government can ultimately gain access to the private keys if deemed necessary.

it's infectious

INFECTIONS FROM THE NET

* Computer viruses are perhaps overhyped in everyday computing environments – but connect your machine to a network of millions of others and the chances of infection increase exponentially.

prevention is better than cure where viruses are concerned

INSIDIOUS WORM

* One of the first major Net infections, and arguably its most notorious to date, happened in November 1988. A virulent worm spread to more than 2,000 host computers on the ARPAnet during an initial attack that lasted for several hours.

* Systems managers found their machines so <u>BOGGED DOWN</u> that they were unable to respond to commands, and eventually the computers crashed. These hosts were being instructed by the worm to make hundreds of connections to other hosts on the Net as it relentlessly tried to spread itself.

* The worm made clever use of anomalies in the Berkeley Unix (BSD) email system to enter the host computers, and used Telnet and the Unix finger utility to copy itself around the network.

ROGUE PROGRAMS

Viruses aren't the only rogue programs. Worms travel through the Net's hinterland, sometimes for good – such as file and email address locators – and sometimes for bad. There are also Trojan horses (programs that look as if they will perform some useful task but contain rogue code) and a multitude of other malignant variations.

er, I think you've got worms!

* And the reason this worm became so notorious? It was programmed and unleashed onto the Net by **Robert T. Morris**, the undergraduate son of the chief scientist at the US National Computer Security Center, **Bob Morris**.

I think it's the notorious worm

vicious worms occasionally propagate themselves over the internet

STRIKE ONE

* Twenty-four hours after the initial strike, systems managers and programmers in the US were still unravelling the worm's code and trying to plug the holes in their ailing computers. Three months later, in January 1990, Morris Jr was CONVICTED under the US's 1986 computer fraud and abuse law.

KEY WORDS

WORM:
Worms are insidious fragments of code which, like viruses, infect computer systems. Worms are able to propagate themselves across networks.

BAITED TRAPS

Over the years there have been some spectacular viruses spread over the Internet, but most take the form of dreary little infections contracted from junk email attachments. Typically, an unsolicited email will invite you to open an attached file that will supposedly tell you about something interesting, or perform some useful function on your machine. Open the attachment, however, and your machine is infected by the virus. The email itself is just the bait: it's the attachment that you need to avoid.

I've got the **anti-virus**

COMBATING VIRUSES

* You can't completely avoid the possibility of infection, but there are some excellent shareware and commercial anti-virus utilities around that will identify most viruses and root them out (see page 189).

anti-virus utilities are available to combat virus attack

computer viruses are best avoided

SENSIBLE PRECAUTIONS

* Unlike the pre-Net years, when anti-virus software quickly became obsolete as new viruses were concocted, today's software can be CONTINUOUSLY UPDATED to include protection against the very latest nasties. You simply browse the Web sites of

'full of vitamin C' 'but will they help my computer avoid viruses?'

the companies who make the software and download PATCH FILES (though always be careful where and what you download – you could be installing rogue code!).

* Other than using anti-virus software, the best step you can take is to make regular back-ups of your computer's files and programs – but don't use a back-up while your computer's hard drive is still infected with a virus, otherwise there's a chance the back-up will be infected too.

take sensible precautions when opening emails

HANDLE WITH CARE

* *Take care when opening emails and attachments*, and delete those which are obviously unsolicited (you'll be able, easily, to tell which they are). Be especially careful with attachments that are Microsoft Word files – it's very easy to create viruses within Microsoft Word macros.

HOAX VIRUSES

Don't believe all the scare stories you come across. There have been a number of famous virus hoaxes sent as warnings in emails.

some viruses are just hoaxes

THAT'S LIFE, JIM

Computer viruses aren't actually alive. They're simply tiny programs that operate independently in the background, copying themselves to your computer and to other machines via infected emails, floppy disks and so on. Some viruses are destructive, but many simply display a silly message before disappearing back into the silicon.

CHAPTER 4
NEWSGROUPS IN ACTION

* Usenet - or 'net news', as it's sometimes called - is the third in the Net's triumvirate of most used services. It's a kind of gigantic electronic bulletin board, divided into many areas of interest (called 'newsgroups') and transmitted all around the globe between Usenet servers. Anyone with access to the Internet can get access to Usenet, read its many articles and post messages of their own.

News or not?

Though it's called news, most of the stuff posted to Usenet consists of personal opinions, pleas for help, announcements (everything from sightings of Elvis to patches for operating systems) and a whole planet's worth of discussion and debate, only a tiny percentage of which will interest you.

and now for the news

net news is not always news

news or not, there's plenty of interest to read on Usenet

HOW USENET BEGAN

* *Usenet grew directly from the openness and the culture of community fostered by Unix.* From the start, the development of Unix had been a collaborative effort involving university computer departments and legions of students.

big news
- I saw ELVIS

all sorts of
stuff gets
posted on Usenet

* It was this policy of openness that led **Tom Truscott** and **Jim Ellis** to tinker with the primitive UUCP networking protocol (which came with every distribution of the Unix operating system) and Unix's batch language, the 'shell script', to create an inter-host news service.

* In the late 1970s Truscott and Ellis were postgraduate students at Duke University, North Carolina. When the university's Unix was upgraded from version VI to VII, the upgrade caused many existing programs to STOP WORKING.

* One such was a data-transfer system known as 'Items', which was used as a primitive bulletin board. Truscott was an ardent supporter of the Unix operating system, having worked during a summer holiday at Bell Labs alongside Unix author **Dennis Ritchie**.

* Along with Ellis, he determined to write a new version of Items that would also surmount its greatest limitation at the time: an inability to deal with items larger than 512 bytes. The pair believed that if they could write a better Items, they could distribute it among Unix user groups and gain for themselves a certain amount of FAME in the Unix community – a cherished prize among Unix hackers.

THE DOWN SIDE OF UPGRADES

Operating-system upgrades often spell the end for programs that depend on foibles in the earlier version in order to work correctly. When an upgrade is introduced with the old foibles ironed out (and usually with new ones ironed in, free of charge), the programs stop working.

FROM ITEMS TO USENET

* Truscott and Ellis discussed their project with fellow postgrads Dennis Rockwell and Steve Bellovin, both Unix enthusiasts. The four of them soon talked up the idea into a much more expansive bulletin board system, able to accept and distribute messages from hundreds of sites using Unix's file system.

KEY WORDS

C:
a bare-bones programming language developed at Bell Laboratories (part of the AT&T telephone company) in the United States and used to write the Unix operating system

X FILES

The first newsgroup names on Usenet were denoted by net.xxx and dept.xxx. These two were followed by fa.xxxx when a gateway between ARPAnet and Usenet was established.

MAPPING OUT A PROTOCOL

* The four mapped out a suitable protocol for message transfer, and Bellovin translated this paper protocol into a three-page Unix shell script to test it. The incredible ease and convenience of Unix shell scripting enabled the Usenet pioneers to implement the early system and considerably shortened its development time. Bellovin's remarkable first shell script allowed for multiple newsgroups, inter-group cross-postings, and lists of subscribers.

* At this point, another Duke postgrad, Steve Daniel, made a significant contribution to the idea. Daniel suggested a format for DELINEATING subject areas, gave them the name 'newsgroups', and introduced

the four mapped out a protocol
for message transfer

the dotted newsgroup hierarchy structure still used today (such as comp.sys.atari.8bit).

✱ Daniel rewrote Bellovin's shell script using the powerful C programming language, and called the fledgling net-news software 'A-News'. One of the first net-news newsgroups was net.chess, devoted to Truscott's other passion – writing chess-playing programs that could beat human players.

GETTING CONNECTED

✱ In 1979 the first sites were connected to Usenet. Not surprisingly, these were Duke University and the University of North Carolina, Bellovin's Alma Mater. Duke Medical School's Physiology Department (PHS) was the third, followed soon after by two sites at Bell Labs.

chess was one of the first Usenet groups

✱ *By the summer of 1980 there were eight hosts attached to Usenet*, and its popularity was growing. The critical point came when **Mark Horton**, a postgraduate student at the University of California at Berkeley, established a link between Usenet and the fledgling mailing lists that were popular at the time on ARPAnet (UCB was an ARPAnet contractor and had a gateway onto the network).

initially Usenet users could read mail but not post it

One-way street

Initially the link between Usenet and the ARPAnet was one way only. Usenet users could read mail from ARPAnet but were unable to post to it because of the 'appropriate use' restrictions imposed by the government. However, Horton persisted and eventually established a feed between the mailing list and Usenet newsgroups. Very quickly the feed created a critical mass of traffic, which acted as an irresistible lure for other sites to join Usenet.

arghh too much news

FROM A-NEWS TO B-NEWS

* By the spring of 1981 Usenet traffic was such that the A-News program was in danger of being unable to cope. Messages had to be read in strict sequence, and the A-News user interface left much to be desired. It was clear that new net-news software was needed.

VACATION PROJECT

* UCB's Mark Horton teamed up with **Matt Glickman**, a local high-school student who was looking for a computer project to fill his spring break from school. Horton was hard at work on his thesis and couldn't spare time for programming, but together they spec'd out what would become B-NEWS. Glickman spent a week writing and bringing up a primitive version.

* Not only did it provide a much improved user interface, the new software enabled articles to be read out of sequence and featured an expiry date so that dated articles would be expunged automatically from the system.

* B-News was released officially in late 1982. Though arguments raged during this time about the validity of newsgroups

by 1981 Usenet traffic was out of control

NET-NEWS PROTOCOL

Where would the Net be without its protocols? Just like every other Net service, Usenet has a protocol all its own – the Net News Transport Protocol (NNTP).

B-news released

B NEWS

B-news was launched in late 1982

devoted to trivial subjects, Usenet remained an uncensored information exchange, free to all who could afford the telephone bills for a UUCP connection.

bills, bills!

NEWSFEED NIGHTMARE

* At the dawn of the 21st century Usenet sports more than 25,000 newsgroups, devoted to any and every topic you can dream up – and many that would feature only in your WORST NIGHTMARES. Popular newsgroups can generate many megabytes of data a day – probably far more than you can realistically download and read.

we aren't pleased with this

Dutch telecommunications companies weren't pleased

The Newsfeed

Usenet is one of the Internet's most used networks. Popular newsgroups can generate several hundred messages a day, though some of the more arcane ones might muster as few as two or three messages a week. Which messages you see depends upon which newsgroups your ISP takes from Usenet and makes available to you – in other words, your 'newsfeed'. Your newsfeed also controls many other aspects of the Usenet service. Some newsfeeds update almost hourly, others take several days and miss out on a lot of postings in between.

GOING DUTCH

Usenet first reached Europe during 1983, when Teus Hagen and Piet Beertema, programmers at the Mathematisch Centrum, a research centre in Amsterdam, established a transatlantic link using a 1,200 baud modem – a device outlawed by the Dutch telecommunications authorities at that time.

FILTERING OUT THE FREAKS

very furtive behaviour

phone phreaking and pirating are both illegal

* Though Usenet is meant to be an entirely uncensored coming together of the world's online communities, many ISPs frequently filter out the less salubrious newsgroups. Principal among these are many weird sex-oriented groups, but there are also newsgroups devoted to the illegal copying of commercial software (pirating) and 'phone phreaking', the practice of tinkering with the telephone system.

local laws apply to newsfeed supplies

Long arm of the law

Bear in mind that just because your newsfeed makes available newsgroups devoted to the unpleasant, that doesn't make them legally viewable. If local laws prohibit an activity that you engage in via a newsgroup, you could make yourself liable to prosecution.

IF YOU WANT TO READ IT ALL...

* *What you feel about this censorship depends largely upon your sexual preferences and belief in 'free' speech* (which on Usenet almost invariably seeks to inhibit someone else's!).
* Your ISP will have its own criteria for censoring its newsfeed, and may decide that certain newsgroups will expire quickly or not be made available to you at all. Nevertheless, there are ways to access all the newsgroups, if you want to do so – by using either dedicated net-news ISPs or Web-based Usenet archives such as Deja.com.

CROSS-POSTINGS

✱ Like the Web, Usenet features hundreds of megabytes of PORNOGRAPHY. Some people rather like the idea, others find it repugnant. The problem is that, unlike the Web, where it's pretty easy to avoid accessing porn sites, Usenet is littered with what are known as cross-postings – messages (usually advertisements) posted to many thousands of newsgroups in one go, whether on-topic or not.

slipped through the net again

ISPs censor newsfeeds, but parents and the delicate should beware: net nasties sometimes slip through

✱ Adverts for sex services, tempters from porn Web sites and lurid invitations from the patently criminally insane make up the biggest part of these cross-postings. The result is that they can unexpectedly turn up in otherwise innocuous newsgroups that are read by CHILDREN or those with delicate sensibilities.

watch what your children watch

Parents beware

As a parent, you can supervise your children's adventures on Usenet, just as you can with other parts of the Net. If your children like to read the postings of, say, a music newsgroup, you can download all the messages in one go and edit them offline, deleting those that are unsuitable before allowing your children to view the rest.

software pirating can be a big problem

it's so
sophisticated

NEWSREADERS

* Usenet is accessed using dedicated 'newsreader' software that organizes the various groups and handles downloads and postings. Microsoft and Netscape

newsreaders can be
full of features

offer newsreaders as part of their well-known browser packages Internet Explorer/Outlook Express and Netscape Navigator. Both of them offer simple, competent access to net news. There are also various independent newsreaders, with lots of sophisticated features but without the convenience of integration.

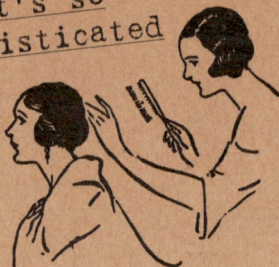

OUTLOOK EXPRESS

* *Bundled with the PC version of Internet Explorer 4.0 is Outlook Express*, a newsreader and email application in one package. Outlook is a competent newsreader with a variety of easy-to-use features.

* The Macintosh version of Explorer also sports a built-in newsreader, which works in much the same way.

Outlook Express comes
all in one package

USENET HIERARCHIES

ALT: weird and wonderful
COMP: computer talk
MISC: everything else
NEWS: news about Usenet
REC: hobbies and pastimes
SCI: science discussions
SOC: social groups
TALK: debate

NETSCAPE NEWSREADERS

* Earlier versions of Netscape Navigator also boasted a built-in newsreader. This works perfectly well, but its interface is deemed CONFUSING by some users, and it doesn't have the bells and whistles of later newsreaders.

and here's your free newsreader

most browsers offer a free newsreader in the package

SEARCH CRITERIA

✱ Netscape's Communicator suite offers a separate newsreader known as <u>COLLABRA</u>, which features many improvements over the earlier Navigator software. Principal among these is a 'Search for a Group' feature, which is useful for locating newsgroups of interest. Enter a key word into a pop-up search dialog and Collabra does the rest, trawling through the thousands of groups and picking out those which match the search criteria. Do this manually once or twice and you'll be very glad of the feature!

'what a good feature this is'

OTHER READERS

For those who don't have Outlook Express or Netscape Communicator, or favour other products, there are many other newsreader applications. For the PC, there's the excellent 'Agent' (PC only) from Forte Inc., which is available, in its Free Agent incarnation, as a free download from Forte's Web site (see pages 188-89). Macintosh users might like to have a look at Newswatcher, a similar program available for download from a variety of sources on the Net (see pages 188-89 for URLs).

I'm looking for people like me

Search for a Group finds newsgroups of interest to you

now say
hello

the first step is to
introduce your
newsreader to your
news server

ACCESSING USENET

* In all cases, the first step in accessing Usenet is to tell your newsreader software the name of your news server. This is supplied by your ISP and will look something like: news.wimpleware.co.uk (note that there's no @ symbol in what otherwise looks very much like an email address)

MANY A MICKLE

You can use your newsreader to browse and read messages interactively while online, or instruct it to download messages along with their headers and then read them offline, thereby saving on telephone charges. The latter is a convenient way to filter out unsuitable messages and cross-postings so that they won't be seen by children. It will also save you money. The only snag is that downloading all the messages from a popular newsgroup can take some time.

THE BIG DOWNLOAD

* The next step is to *access the news server for the first time and download a complete listing of the newsgroups* available to you. The process will undoubtedly take some time (perhaps 20 minutes or so), but once the groups are downloaded you can browse and read those which the news server keeps on line. However, for some of the more obscure groups, you may have to make an explicit request to your ISP.

BROWSING AND POSTING

As you browse through the headers in a newsgroup, a simple click (sometimes a double-click) will open

browsing through
newsgroup headers
can be fun

each one and display its message on screen. At this point you can reply by posting to the group directly, either by email or by clicking the appropriate button or selecting the option you want from a menu, depending on which newsreader application you're using.

postings can take a while to provide a response

pssst pass it on

don't expect too speedy a response as messages can take quite a while to be circulated around a group

* When you post to a group, your message is echoed back to you when you REFRESH the list of headers (i.e. cause the newsreader to access the news server and download any new headers). However, it might take your message a day or more to be circulated throughout the Usenet network, so don't expect an instant response to a post.

SUBSCRIPTION SERVICE

All the popular newsreader programs enable you to subscribe to your favourite groups. This means that the next time you run the software you'll be presented with a convenient list of the groups to which you've subscribed (it doesn't mean that these newsgroups will be sent directly to your computer). What subscribing does is to provide you with a shortcut to your favourite newsgroups, so you don't have to trawl through the huge list of newsgroups (currently 25,000 or more) to find those you like every time you want to read them.

don't ask me
AGAIN!

QUESTIONS
AND ANSWERS

* Almost every news-group has its own FAQ - list of Frequently Asked Questions - offering answers to questions that 'newbies' (those new to the group) are most likely to ask. Asking and answering these questions time and again

newsgroups have their own way
of offering answers to the most
frequently asked questions

wastes bandwidth, is considered poor 'netiquette', and will probably invoke a sharp response from the less patient of the group's regulars.

KEY WORDS

FAQ:
Frequently Asked Questions – a list of commonly asked questions, complete with answers

FAQS ON FILE

* *Sometimes the FAQ is posted to the newsgroup itself on a regular basis by the group's moderator* or someone else appointed to the task. Occasionally a Web site address is given for the FAQ. As a newbie, you should take the trouble to read the FAQ, as it will answer most of your initial questions and, perhaps more importantly, give a feel for how the group is conducted.

* If the FAQ doesn't have the information you want, post to the newsgroup with the qualifier that you've read the FAQ but can't find an answer to the question that's troubling you.

IT'S A WASTE

don't keep asking the
same questions

✱ Though FAQs usually contain SOLID INFORMATION, occasionally they're simply the opinions of people it's pretty safe to ignore. As with anything else you read, trust your own instincts!

ATTACHMENTS

✱ Many Usenet messages are posted with attachments such as a picture, sound, animation, or sometimes an entire program. These are almost invariably in STANDARD FILE FORMATS, such as JPG or GIF for picture files and AVI or MPEG for animation and movies, or in one of the many popular compression formats for binary files.

need to know an answer? look in the central index of FAQs

CATALOGUE OF FAQS

A central index of FAQs is maintained by the Massachusetts Institute of Technology (you can find it at ftp://rtfm.mit.edu/pub/usenet-by-hierarchy).

WEIRD!

On Usenet, you'll see lots of words that end in 'z' and ones that have deliberately weird misspellings or strange capitals letters in the middle – WaRez (pirate software), pHreAKerz (people who tamper with the phone system), and so on. These postings come from self-styled cyberpunks who want to make you think that they're cool techno-jockeys able to bend the Net to their will.

it's perfectly okay to ignore opinions that you read in FAQs

✱ Most newsreaders will handle pictures, sound and movies AUTOMATICALLY, displaying them either inline along with the message or in a separate window after you've elected to view the attachment from an option in the main program, or by launching helper software.

THE HAZARDS OF USENET

✱ You need to take extreme care when opening attachments from some newsgroups - particularly controversial groups devoted to 'WaRez', virus issues and the like. Always check files from suspect sources by scanning them with an anti-virus program.

take care when opening attachments

SPAMMERS, TROLLS AND LURKERS

✱ When many people come together to share their views you can be sure that some of them will have some WEIRD NOTIONS of how to behave or what constitutes an acceptable posting.

✱ The most notorious kind of post is 'SPAM' – commercial advertising or other inappropriate messages dressed up as information. A few years ago, spammers would attract the full WRATH of Usenet's devoted posters and be deluged with angry messages from the self-righteous. Nowadays, commercial Internet activity is such that spam is commonplace. A waste of bandwidth, it is an irritation best ignored.

✱ TROLLS – people who make provocative postings to incite flame wars (see pages 52-53) – are largely ignored nowadays, too. After a few months online to Usenet, you'll

KEY WORDS

TROLL:
someone who makes provocative postings ('flame bait') in a deliberate attempt to incite a flame war

I'd like some spam please

does anyone really like spam?

140

have seen every possible combination of human stupidity, so what could possibly encourage you to respond to yet another bit of flame bait?

✱ LURKERS are people who browse Usenet messages without contributing anything. Such non-participation was once viewed as an antisocial act – though in some cases it can be a blessing!

there's a bit missing

often bits of a multi-part file are missing

USENET BEHAVIOUR

✱ *More than any other Net service, Usenet has a code of conduct it's wise to follow.* True, being flamed in any great way is increasingly rare nowadays, but breaches of netiquette are likely to provoke sharp comments from other posters and you may lose credibility to such an extent that you can no longer make useful postings.

✱ Nevertheless, though most people abide by Usenet etiquette, many ignore it completely, make frequent cross-postings, and swear at other posters or call them names.

Multi-part postings

Some large files – such as movies and applications software – are split into what are known as multi-part binary postings. They can be recognized as a sequence of posts in a newsgroup all with the same name but with part numbers appended to them. For example:

Winona in a bikini – win.jpg (01/05)
Winona in a bikini – win.jpg (02/05)
Winona in a bikini – win.jpg (03/05)

... and so on. You need to download all the parts in order to reconstruct the original file. Often you'll find that one or more parts of a really big multi-part file is missing. This is annoying and can occur for a number of reasons, such as your ISP expiring part of the post. Check through the headers of multi-part postings, and if one part is missing don't bother to download the rest.

but I never contribute

lurkers are people who read but don't contribute

LATEST
READ ALL ABOUT IT

DEJANEWS

* You may find that
your ISP offers a cut-
down newsfeed, or that
articles are expired before
you've had a chance to read
them. Both situations are
irksome: some people are

people wanted
personalised news

interested in topics other than wine, film and the
doings of Microsoft, and not everyone is able to
log on several times a day to catch up with the
latest posts.

I want good
behaviour
at all times

it is good to follow
the code of conduct

FREE FORM

Feel free to ignore the
code of conduct advice
if it suits you – plenty
of other users do!
Though think twice
before being unkind.

ARCHIVING NEWS

* To get around the problem, you can
access one of the Web-based Usenet
archivers. *The best and most widely known
is DejaNews* (see pages 94-95), which has
archived Usenet postings since 1995.
Using DejaNews is free, though you have
to put up with a certain amount of
advertising.

IRRITATING PAUSES

* Until recently, the advertisements
didn't interfere with the process of reading
newsgroups. However, a reorganization has
led to distinct and rather irritating pauses,
after advertising banners have loaded and
before messages and headers are displayed.
This occurs every time you click on a
message or a follow-up posting. The screen
clears, then an advertising banner is

downloaded and displayed – followed by a palpable and <u>ANNOYING</u> pause to enable you to read the ad before the message.

✱ However, even annoying pauses are better than not being able to read a newsgroup at all because your ISP doesn't offer it or quickly expires its messages.

@!✱!

don't write in capital letters unless you want to imply shouting

BEAT THE CLOCK

✱ If you find the pauses between the advertisements and the messages irritating, try clicking your browser's 'Stop' button a few seconds after an ad has appeared. This will shorten the pause and cause the message to be displayed. The click has to be timed just right, through– or you'll interrupt the transmission of the message itself and have to reload it, which is even more irritating!

sorry!

if necessary, include an apology in your posting

Net-news netiquette

Read the newsgroup's FAQs and try only to make on-topic postings. If you do stray from the subject matter, include an apology in your posting. Ignore cross-posts from other posters. There's no point in using up further bandwidth by ticking off cross-posters and spammers, who probably couldn't care less. Don't quote entire postings in your answers. It's a waste of bandwidth. Be aware that some posters might not be able to muster your level of literacy, and that pointing out that fact is ungracious in the extreme. If you feel you must post a sharp response, take a deep breath first. Don't write with capital letters – unless you want to imply shouting.

143

USING DEJANEWS

* To use DejaNews, point your browser at http://www.deja.com/. Enter the name of a newsgroup into the search field provided and DejaNews will display the most recent messages associated with the group. If Deja can't find the newsgroup you want (because you've entered the name incorrectly) or if you enter a key word rather than a newsgroup name, DejaNews will provide you with a list of newsgroups that most closely match your search criteria. Select one of them by clicking on it, and its recent postings will be displayed.

INDEPENDENT NEWSGROUPS

There are many newsgroups that operate on networks independent of Usenet. Some are oriented towards news and information local to you, others are aimed at satisfying the needs of users of particular products or services. Examples include the gnu network for Unix aficionados, eunet delivering European news, and UK-specific services such as uk.events, which details happenings around the UK.

with DejaNews there is no need to rely on a carrier pigeon for personalized news

PERSONALIZED SERVICE

* *It's also possible to register for a personalized account* with DejaNews (a service called MyDejaNews). Registration is straightforward and free and, as a bonus, you'll be given a free mailbox too.

* A MyDejaNews account enables you to subscribe to the newsgroups you like to read regularly, so that they're ready for you to click and peruse whenever you log into the service.

check on his author profile

you can
track people
down using
an author
profile

IT COULD BE YOU!

* As well as news and mail, DejaNews also provides an interesting 'AUTHOR PROFILE' service. This enables anyone to check the posting history of any Usenet poster. Type a name into Deja's search engine and all of that person's postings dating back to 1995 will be displayed, along with his or her email address.

* As you might imagine, author profiles are potentially EMBARRASSING. It could be that someone out there will want to profile you – so always post with care!

I get special news on mine

DejaNews makes news
individually
relevant

Profiles

Author profiles make it easy to trawl back through the postings of the people you find interesting. This is also a useful way to locate postings from people who are experts in their field, or to track down email addresses (in fact, email-address directories use this method).

I need to work on my
author profile

STARTING A NEWSGROUP

* How are newsgroups established? Via a complex process of announcements and voting, in an attempt to establish a ground swell of popularity for the proposed newsgroup.

newsgroups are started by a process of voting and nomination

KEY WORDS

HIERARCHY: A Usenet category

STRING: A sentence or other sequence of ASCII characters

CONTROL TEXT STRING: A string used to command a service or computer

is there a **shortcut**

there are shortcuts to setting up but they have drawbacks

Help pages devoted to creating newsgroups are available on the Web (see page 186 for URLs).

DEMOCRATIC PROCESS

* *It's difficult, though not impossible, to start a group of your own* – though the difficulties involved in fact work in favour of Usenet, by keeping potentially unpopular or useless groups out (based on how many or how few people want them, not on whether people agree with their subject matter), thereby maximizing bandwidth for the popular groups.

* To CREATE A NEWSGROUP, decide under which hierarchy the group will reside. Most hierarchies have a .config newsgroup, which is where you post proposals for new groups.

* Obviously, you'll need to prepare a POTENT ARGUMENT for the creation of the new group. Take your time over this, so that your proposal is convincing and valid. You'll also need to choose a suitable name (you'll be able to divine what is 'suitable' by browsing the names of other groups in the hierarchy).

* Now post your proposal to the .config newsgroup. Others will vote on your proposal (via a convoluted route) and, if you receive at least twice as many 'yes' votes as 'no' votes, and if there are at least 100 more 'yes' votes than 'no' votes, then the group is established.

thou shalt not
have a newsgroup

visit me I'm interesting

you have to entice people to visit your newsgroup

SHORTCUT TO NOWHERE?

* Alternatively, you can start a newsgroup in the 'alt' (all kinds of topics) hierarchy simply by posting a suitable CONTROL TEXT STRING in a special message. The only problem will be how to get people to visit and post to your newsgroup.

AVOIDING DUPLICATION

Before attempting to start a newsgroup of your own, check Usenet itself to see whether one catering to your interests has recently been created. The process of creation is continuous, and there are newsgroups devoted solely to listing the new ones. To find out whether similar groups already exist, you can instruct your newsreader to refresh its database of groups and then try a key word search of the database (some newsreaders offer to download and display new newsgroups each time you log on). Alternatively, you can read the news.lists newsgroup for an up-to-date picture of Usenet.

147

CHAPTER 5

ELECTRONIC GADGETRY

* As you might imagine, there's a lot of underlying physical gadgetry that powers the Internet, though much of it is relatively simple to understand, even for the computer novice. The Internet, as we saw in the Introduction, is an interconnected network of networks based upon a scheme for transmitting data known as packet switching, which was devised by several computer scientists working in parallel (but more or less independently) in the early 1960s.

talk to me

computers were learning to communicate

FATAL FLAWS

Message switching offered a great leap forward in network technology over circuit switching, but has two important flaws. Long messages monopolize a connection for the duration of transmission and may therefore exclude other messages. Also, very large messages can outstrip the node resources required to store and forward them, and so may get lost.

CIRCUITOUS ROUTES

* The first attempts at getting computers to talk to each other made use of direct connections between computers in the same room or building. These experiments developed into computers in different locations being linked together using 'circuit switching' on the public telephone network.

things were hard before packet switching

it's gone
crazy!

✱ Circuit switching is a way of creating a single ELECTRICAL PATHWAY between two entities, whether it be computers or telephone subscribers. Electromechanical equipment at the telephone exchanges switch lines into a continuous path, until the telephone of one of the subscribers is eventually connected to that of the other. They can then communicate.

electrical noise sends the average computer batty

NOISY, SLOW AND EXPENSIVE

✱ Although this appears to be a reasonable solution, it is in fact INEFFICIENT and results in poor-quality transmissions. The line has to be used exclusively by the two people communicating, and the circuit-switching equipment introduces masses of electrical 'noise' to the circuit. This noise can be easily filtered out by the human ear but throws the average computer into a tizzy!

✱ There are other disadvantages, too. Equipment costs are comparatively high and, in computer terms, circuits take a long time to be established – a few seconds is an aeon to a computer that typically operates in millionths of a second.

✱ Circuit switching did, however, prove the feasibility of linking computers; and building on the idea, scientists hit upon a superior scheme, called message switching, using a dedicated partial network of connections between minicomputer nodes.

THE NEXT STEP

With message switching, the host computers are connected to the nodes and the nodes act as switches, routing messages across the network. Any node can communicate with any other node, though not necessarily by a direct connection. There's no electrical noise, because switching is 'logical' rather than physical; hosts may communicate at different speeds, because the node network provides buffering; and there's no time delay in setting up a connection. Messages can be sent even when a host isn't ready to receive them ('store and forward').

A SOLUTION IN A PACKET

psst,
I've got the
solution

* Eventually, the message-switching theory was refined into what became packet switching. This also uses a partially connected network of nodes, but messages are broken into small, discrete packets. Each bears a destination address and can be routed across the network using the most convenient pathway at any given time.

the solution came in the sending of small packages of information

the modem is an electronic sign reader

PASS THE PARCEL

* *Packets are received by a node and reassembled into a message before being passed to the host.* Small packets mean that network resources are managed more efficiently. The packets can also be interleaved easily, leading to the multiplexing of messages and the maximizing of the all-important bandwidth.

* On the fledgling Internet, the nodes became IMPs (Interface Message Processors), joined together to form a partially connected mesh. Each node could have up to four hosts connected to it.

* *A host could pass a message of up to 8K to its node*, which then broke up the message into 1K packets and delivered them across the network. If a host wanted to send a message larger than 8K, it had to break it up into 8K packets before passing them to the node; the receiving host would then reassemble the 8K packets into a message.

BILINGUAL TRANSLATION

* A modem is a kind of <u>ELECTRONIC INTERPRETER</u> that speaks two languages – digital and analogue. The signals present inside a computer are <u>DIGITAL</u>: values are represented by positive and negative voltages, which result in what's called a square wave, an on-again-off-again signal that represents two states.

Sine wave

Square wave

sine waves represent analogue signals, square waves are digital signals

* In the physical world, signals are almost invariably <u>ANALOGUE</u>. An analogue signal is one that is continually varying and can potentially represent an infinite range of values. The analogue signal is called a sine wave.

a modem is a bridge between the computer and the telephone

Bridging device

The modem is at the heart of almost all typical dial-up connections to the Internet using a desktop computer and an ISP. The modem is the device that forms a bridge between the computer and the telephone line, allowing data to pass from the one via the other to your ISP and, ultimately, to the Internet.

ANALOGUE AND DIGITAL

* Digital signals can be used to represent analogue signals. This is achieved by a technique known as 'quantization' or, more commonly nowadays, 'sampling'. The continuous analogue signal is examined - 'sampled' - many times to form a list of discrete values. If these values are played back at the speed at which they were sampled, a fairly accurate representation of the original analogue signal is created.

HI-FI

Digital sampling takes place when you play a music CD. The music itself is analogue, but it has been sampled at a high rate and stored in digital form – a bit pattern – on the CD. These bits are processed during playback and the result is music. Clearly the more samples taken from the original signal, the more accurate the resulting digital representation. Low sample rates result in a low degree of 'fidelity' (faithfulness to the original). High sample rates fool the ear – or eye, with digital video – and produce a high-fidelity (hi-fi) playback.

RELEVANT SIGNALS

* Domestic telephones use analogue signals to represent the human voice. This makes sense because the voice itself is an analogue signal – a pressure wave – which for the purposes of transmission is translated into an electromagnetic wave.

digital
sampling is
what music
CDs use

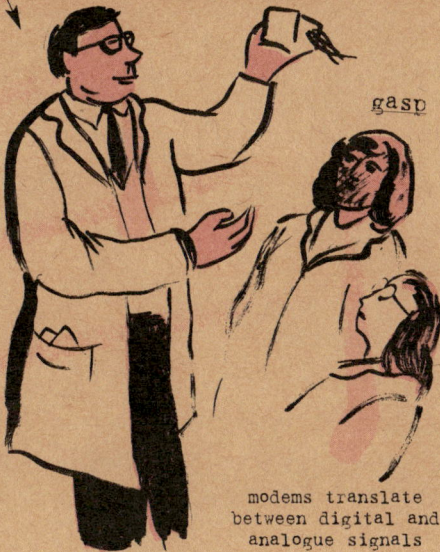

scientist

it's a
miracle

gasp

modems translate
between digital and
analogue signals

KEY WORDS

BIT:
concatenation of
'binary digit' – the
smallest unit of
information
DIGITAL:
analogue data broken
down into tiny
individual samples
MODULATE:
to transmit

✱ Computers, however, don't talk analogue. Their medium is the digital signal. They represent data digitally, by means of a BINARY SYSTEM using electrical 'ons' and 'offs'. For a computer to communicate across the telephone network, some kind of device is necessary to transform its digital 'signal' into an analogue one suitable for transmission and to decode that signal at the receiving end.

A TALKING MIRACLE

✱ The MODEM fulfils this role. The word 'modem' is a contraction of two words – MOdulator and DEModulator – to create a name that effectively describes what the device does. A modem modulates an analogue signal with a digital one, and strips off the digital signal – demodulates it – at the receiving end.

**CONVERGENT
TECHNOLOGY**

At the end of the 1980s the UK's telephone network was converted at great expense from analogue technology to a digital system called System X. Although telephones continued to pass analogue signals to the exchange, they were then converted into digital signals by the exchange and transmitted over the network using a method known as 'pulse code modulation' – essentially, the breaking up of signals into discrete pieces to maximize bandwidth and fidelity (in other words, a telephonic version of packet switching).

geeky
types

careful, that
cost a lot

THE INS AND OUTS OF MODEMS

* Modems come in all shapes and sizes. The most obvious differences, however, are whether the device is external (a separate box that sits alongside your desktop machine) or internal (a plug-in card that fits inside it) and the range of transmission speeds offered by the device.

external modems
cost a lot

INTERNAL V. EXTERNAL

* You connect an EXTERNAL modem to your desktop computer by a cable that plugs into the computer's I/O port. An external modem has its own power supply, usually a DC transformer that plugs into the mains. As well as the cable linking it to the computer, there's one to connect the device to a telephone socket; and sometimes a socket into which you can plug a telephone (if you don't have a socket doubler). If the modem can handle voice messaging, faxes and so on, then there are connectors for adding microphones and speakers, too.

* An INTERNAL modem plugs into an expansion slot inside a PC. It usually has a connector to link it to a telephone socket. There's no need for a power supply,

because the modem is powered directly by the computer. Similarly, data is transferred directly though the expansion slot.

* **External modems are expensive compared with internal modems**, which are stripped down to little more than a bare expansion card. Internal modems dispense with cables and sockets, and offer

'oh, but I need to go direct'

if only I had a **proper modem**

acoustic couplers are very low-tech modems and suffer badly from extraneous noise

stable data transfer via a direct connection. However, they can be used only with PC compatibles. If you're a Mac user, or have one of the 16-bit computers popular a few years ago, such as an Atari ST or a Commodore Amiga, you have to use an external modem.

ACOUSTIC COUPLERS

Direct-connect modems (ones that plug directly into a telephone socket) were preceded by 'acoustic couplers'. These are low-speed modems sporting a couple of rubber cups into which you place a telephone's handset. Modulated tones are relayed to the handset through the rubber cups, in much the same way as you yourself would talk and listen on the phone. Acoustic couplers suffer badly from extraneous noise, and are therefore severely limited in their operating speeds. They have now been largely abandoned, but can still be useful for connecting to telephones that don't have a socket, such as the ones in public phone booths or some hotel bedrooms.

MODEM SPEEDS

* The first widely available modems communicated at a speed of 300 baud, though a split baud rate of 75/1,200 was popular in the UK for a while. It was reasoned that most users couldn't type terribly well and therefore wouldn't need to transmit at much above 75 baud, but would benefit from receiving data from other computers at the faster speed.

speed is
jolly important
with a modem

KEY WORDS

BAUD RATE:
A measure of the speed of modem communications, named after J.M.E. Baudot (1845-1903), inventor of a 5-bit electric telegraphy code (known as the International Telegraph Alphabet No.2). Baud rate is roughly equal to bits per second (bps), though the difference is significant at higher speeds (because Baud rate measures signalling elements per second not bits per second).

FROM 300 TO 2,400 BAUD

* *Early 300-baud modems were operated manually.* That is, the user had to select the mode of operation using a knob on the front of the device, dial the number of a desired service, and then set the modem to communicate after hearing a tone from the other end.

early modems were
operated by hand

156

I want the **fastest** *you've got*

* Later models offered AUTOMATIC operation. They were able to dial, negotiate an operating speed and begin communicating – all controlled by software on the host computer. Some modems, known as 'autodial/autoanswer', were also able to detect a calling modem automatically and then answer the phone. These more sophisticated gadgets enabled users to set up the first unattended electronic bulletin boards run on personal computers.

* Soon 1,200-baud modems became widespread, and the consensus at the time (the mid-1980s) was that this speed was probably the fastest feasible using ordinary domestic telephone lines. But this assumption was quickly proved wrong – when a method was devised to enable modems to achieve a truly staggering 2,400 baud, by technical trickery.

AND NOW MANY TIMES FASTER

* And so to the present, when the fastest modems available communicate at 56K baud (compare with the 2.4K rate of only a few years ago), using clever proprietary protocols developed by several manufacturers.

* In fact, the 56K 'standard' is actually a kind of split baud rate. You transmit to the ISP using a speed of 33K baud and receive at 56K when line conditions allow (infrequently, it must be said). A PRACTICAL MAXIMUM appears to be somewhere around 45K.

Best price

Price plays a part in choosing a faster modem. A device that offers 56K will be more expensive than one that can manage, say, 28K. However, a faster operating speed equates directly to a saving on phone bills.

HIGH-TECH TELEPHONY

A new(ish) standard for telephone line transmission is ISDN – short for Integrated Services Digital Network, a system that has abandoned analogue communications in favour of the digital variety. Because ISDN telephone lines use digital signals only, there's no need for digital to analogue conversion. The result is much higher transmission speeds (typically 128K baud) and greater fidelity.

THE 'V' SIGN

* Not a rude gesture, but a standard way to specify a modem's speed rating. The 56K standard is known as V90 - or rather, one of the 56K standards, the others being X2 and 56Kflex - while 28K is known as V34 and 14K as V32bis (the nomenclature was devised by the French, hence the 'bis').

okay where are those lost files?

the V sign is a way to specify a modem's speed

compression helps files to stay together

Don't get lost

Compression is used to reduce the number of bytes in a file and speed through-put in data transmissions. But it is also used for a more esoteric purpose: to bring together programs and their associated configuration and support files into a single compressed archive, so that it can be transmitted as one continuous block – rather than as a collection of files, some of which might get lost in the process.

THE EFFECTS OF COMPRESSION

* *Another V standard is used alongside the measurement of speed*, namely V42 – the standard for data compression and error checking.

* COMPRESSION enables large files to be crunched down into smaller ones, effectively increasing the speed of transmission. This is why modem manufacturers, ISPs and others can advise you to set your computer to communicate at, say, 115K, when the maximum speed of your modem is only 56K. Compression narrows the gap.

QUART IN A PINT POT

* Data compression is used throughout computer communications at various levels. When you download files from an

FTP server, they've almost invariably been compressed using one of the 'standard' formats such as Zip or StuffIt. Compression is also available at the hardware level of a modem. Modern modems compress and decompress data on the fly (using a system known as MNP or <u>MIRACOM NETWORK PROTOCOL</u> after the company which devised it) as it's passed to them from the host computer, prior to transmitting it over the telephone line.

it's responding to compression very well

FIT FILES

some files respond to compression better than others

✳ Some files respond exceedingly well to compression, whereas ones that are already stored in a kind of compressed format (such as the JPG image file format) do not, since redundancy has already been removed from them to a great degree.

Reductions

How is it possible to reduce the size of a file and rebuild it at the receiving end? Compression relies on seeking out redundant bytes of data within the file. 'Redundant' is defined as being a sequence of three or more of the same bytes. Take, for example, five occurrences of the letter 'J', which in ASCII is 74 74 74 74 74. A compression algorithm would substitute just one 'J' for this sequence, count how many 'J's must be put back in order to rebuild the file, and express it as 74 05. When the decompressing software encounters this sequence, it realizes that it must replace the 74 05 sequence with five bytes of 74.

'we've got big reductions today madam'

WHAT MODEMS UNDERSTAND

* Most modems are now controlled by means of a simple programming language. At first modems used incompatible proprietary languages, but modem manufacturers soon hit upon a standard: the Hayes command language.

%

it's a very smart modem

the modem smart set

'ATTENTION, PLEASE!'

* The US company D.C. Hayes & Co. is a modem manufacturer, just like any other. *Unlike the others, however, Hayes' elegant modem-control language pioneered the concept of smart modems* able to be controlled automatically by a host computer. Its subsequent success in the marketplace led others to adopt the Hayes language for their modems, making them instantly compatible with the popular communications software.

* Today, almost all modems use at least a subset of the Hayes commands. The language is known as the AT COMMAND SET, because its core command is 'AT' – short for 'attention' (i.e. 'Modem, give me your attention!').

CHAIN OF COMMAND

* The letters AT are supplemented by a variety of single-letter commands, which can be combined with control characters

% & ?

okay class
attention

ATDT
1234 9876

'I wish
I was
smart'

The at for 'attention' command is the most
basic in the Hayes modem lexicon

such as &, % and \ to create command
sequences. To make the modem dial a
number, for example, you would issue the
command ATDT 1234 9876 (in which AT

means attention, D
means dial, and T
means tone dial).
You could
substitute P for
pulse dial; or omit
the P or T, in which
case the modem
will dial using

'attention, can you
speak hayes?'

whatever default method has been
programmed into its firmware (almost
invariably tone dialling nowadays).

SERIAL IN 232 PARTS

I do love a good serial

* An external modem is connected using a standardized computer I/O port variously known as an RS232 port or serial port or sometimes by its CCITT designation, V24. In serial communications, data is passed one bit after another along a single 'line'. Compare with parallel communication (such as the Centronics 'standard' for printers), where several bits are transmitted at the same time along parallel lines. Although serial communications are often slower than parallel communications, they are cheaper to implement and more stable over longer distances.

it's the eternal triangle

ETERNAL TRIANGLE

* *Just three lines are required to establish a serial link* – transmit, receive and signal ground. But a typical serial port features many more lines, to provide extra features such as the ability to detect a calling modem or a 'carrier' signal on the telephone line, and so on.

VARIATIONS ON A THEME

* Many computers feature variations on the RS232 theme. Some, such as Apple's Macintosh, use different connectors; some use RS432, an uprated version of RS232; and still others

three lines are required to establish a serial link

MODEM JARGON

External modems often feature a number of LEDs that indicate various states in the transmission process. Although they're usually labelled, the abbreviations rarely make much sense to novices. However, these indicators can be a big help if you're trying to resolve a problem.

MR: Modem Ready. Active when the modem is switched on and in a state that is ready to receive instructions from the host computer.

CD: Carrier Detect. Active when the modem has detected a signal from a remote computer/modem.

TD/TX: Active when the modem is transmitting data.

RD/RX: Active when the modem is receiving data.

OH: Off Hook. Active when the modem has 'picked up' the telephone line and is ready to dial a number and establish communications.

HS: High Speed: Active when the modem is operating at speeds greater than 4,800bps.

AA: Auto Answer. Active when the modem is ready to receive incoming calls automatically (when it's being used to power a personal bulletin board, for example).

have their own hybrid serial ports. One common variation is to offer TTL (5V) signals, rather than the full 12V RS232 signals.

MAKING CONNECTIONS

★ *The standard connector for serial communications is a 25-pin D-type connector*, and this is still used almost exclusively on external modems. However, modern PC-like computers now mostly have a 9-pin connector (first adopted for the IBM PC-AT computer). This 9-pin connector offers a subset of the standard RS232 lines that is adequate for most everyday situations.

carriers contain computer communications

CHAPTER 6
GETTING ONLINE TO THE WORLD

is it really that easy?

* Reading about the Internet is all very well, but sooner or later you'll want to make a connection and explore it all for yourself. Fortunately, rapid evolution in both the Net and the software used to explore it means that it's no longer necessary to have a degree in computer science to get online.

'I can't wait to go world wide!'

OPEN TO ENHANCEMENT

When it was launched in the early 1980s, the PC's 'open architecture' created a mini-revolution in computing. At a time when other computer manufacturers all but hermetically sealed their machines, so fear of invalidating the warranty deterred owners from tinkering within, IBM's personal computer positively throbbed with third-party add-ons.

GET GOING

* *To get online, you'll need an account with an Internet Service Provider (ISP), a computer with the appropriate software, a telephone line and a modem*. With these and an hour or so at your disposal, you can get connected to the Net.

WHICH COMPUTER

* For those yet to acquire a computer, the choice is bewildering. PCs of every conceivable size, shape and configuration abound. There's a dazzling and ever changing array of Apple Macs. And you can find countless brands of computers, all almost entirely INCOMPATIBLE with each other, available second-hand. For Internet use, which do you choose?
* Although there are computers with arguably better specifications, the

ubiquitous IBM PC and lookalikes has long been the first choice for virtually any application, for many compelling reasons.

✳ Introduced way back in the early 1980s as IBM's entry into the home computer market, the PC benefited from its open architecture. It was easy to install peripheral plug-in hardware inside the machine, making it easy to upgrade, thus staving off obsolescence.

there is a dazzling array
of computers for sale

✳ IBM's PC quickly DOMINATED the market. Corporate buyers looking for desktop machines bought it in droves. The resulting installed user base led to ever more software houses developing products to support the machine, which led to more people buying it, and so the cycle continued.

KEY WORDS

SYSTEM SOFTWARE: (also called the operating system or OS) the software that controls the operation of a computer at 'system level' – its disk drives, screen display and so on

Doppelgangers

With the advent of PC clones – cheaper computers from third-party manufacturers that behaved like PCs, being operated in the same way and running the same software – world dominance of the desktop-computer market was just a mouse click away.

Unequal choice

Today, the PC is still the first choice for those yet to buy a computer. If you're buying one with a view to joining the Internet, the variety of compatible software and cheap add-on hardware, coupled with complete Internet support, should make for easy connection and trouble-free use.

THE MAC AND THE OTHERS

* Unlike the PC, Apple's Macintosh computer was designed to use a point-and-click operating system from the start - in fact, it was its chief selling point. Although breathtakingly expensive when launched, the Mac gradually became cheaper as it competed with the PC for an ever more discriminating market, eventually enabling home as well as business users to buy the Mac.

KEY WORDS

COMMAND-LINE INTERFACE:
OS controlled by keyword instructions

EASY OR DIFFICULT?

Although the process of going online is still very much geared to PCs, owners of newer Apple Macintosh computers will find the operation fairly easy, too. For the rest of the population (owners of Atari STs, Commodore Amigas, Acorn computers et al), getting online is a rather more difficult experience – but it is possible, and owners of these machines should not be deterred.

computers became commonplace

ATARI AND THE REST

* *The Macintosh came to dominate the world of publishing and print*, where its GUI (point-and-click) front-end – at a time when all other machines used a command-line interface – made on-screen page make-up an easy task.
* When home and small-business computing really got going in the 1980s,

many manufacturers offered computers to the buying public and some enjoyed immense popularity. The Commodore Amiga, Atari's ST, the Acorn Archimedes and one or two others all used proprietary operating systems with GUI FRONT-ENDS that looked, for a while, like challenging the dominance of the PC.

✱ With the exception of small bands of diehard enthusiasts, all these machines have more or less faded from view, though the Acorn Archimedes is still popular in some schools and colleges. However, the Amiga, Archimedes and ST can all be successfully connected to the Internet.

✱ And preceding even these now ancient pieces of silicon were the 8-bit home computers, many of which have loyal bands of followers to this day. The best ones belong to the ATARI 8-BIT range – real computers, with a real operating system and plenty of peripherals. You can use them to connect to the Internet, though the experience won't be quite as exciting as surfing with the latest PC or Mac. But, unlike them, Atari 8-bits can be picked up for a few pounds at car-boot and jumble sales and the software to drive them is freely available from the Internet (ask a friend with an Internet account to download it for you).

small bands of enthusiasts take old machines online

HISTORIC CONNECTION

It seems amazing that it's possible to connect an ancient Atari 8-bit computer to the Net. But if you've got one or are able to acquire one in working order cheaply, why not check out Ken Siders' Project ICE home page (URL on page 189) for free software and do just that?

'it's amazing what we used to do with our Atari 8-bits'

what a bargain

dig out a machine
and away you go

SUPPORT FOR OLD WORKHORSES

Enthusiasts of older or alternative computers will find a wealth of support for them on the Internet, where diehard fans form themselves into pressure groups devoted to keeping their machines alive.

it's a
bargain madam

there are plenty of
software and hardware
bargains to be found

ACQUIRING SOFTWARE

* Whichever computer you choose, it will need suitable software to connect it to the Internet. Recent PCs almost invariably come with Windows, and both Windows 95 and Windows 98 feature integrated Internet software that handles all aspects of connecting. Apple Macs are also well supported, with both commercial and shareware Internet software.

GETTING IT FROM THE NET

* *Locating software for other computers is possible, but requires slightly more effort.* Paradoxically, the Internet itself is the best place to look for suitable software – and that means either asking a friend already on the Net to download it for you or making use of a connection at work, school or college, or perhaps a visit to a cybercafé (see page 184). You'll need some sort of <u>STORAGE DEVICE</u> (such as an Iomega Zip drive or a Syquest drive) in order to transfer the software to your own computer.

BARGAINS GALORE

* With a little spare cash and a burning desire to get connected, a <u>SECOND-HAND</u>

computer is the solution. The ceaseless advances in computer hardware have meant a short life span for many machines, rapidly made redundant as their owners upgrade. These machines can be had cheaply from second-hand shops, small ads in newspapers, charity shops, and even CAR-BOOT SALES.

'I'm just longing for a pocket pal'

I'm surfin'

you can get online anytime, anywhere with a pocket pal at your side

✱ PCs PENSIONED OFF in favour of the latest machines make excellent second-hand purchases. Very early PCs – those with an Intel 8088 or 8086 processor – can be acquired for just a few pounds, or sometimes even for free, when friends, neighbours and relatives have a clear-out. Even this silicon from the dark ages can be put to use in order to access the Net!

POCKET PALS

As well as all sorts of desktop computers and their laptop counterparts, a whole breed of pocket computers has evolved during the past five years or so. Initially little more than electronic diaries, these machines have developed to the point where they can be put to useful work accessing email, browsing newsgroups and even surfing the Web, all with the convenience that pocket size brings. With a portable telephone, you can access the Internet wherever you are – even on the beach!

you can get online for just a few pounds

169

CHOOSING AN ISP

* What kind of ISP you choose depends on how much you want to pay for an account, how much hand-holding you want, whether censorship is an issue, and so on.

the very important piggy is your ISP

and the internet please

get online at the supermarket

PIGGY IN THE MIDDLE

Once you've got a computer, a modem and suitable software on your desktop, all you now need is an account with an ISP in order to go online. ISPs come in all shapes and sizes. Some of them offer straightforward connection to the Net as their primary business; some, such as AOL and CompuServe, evolved from giant public-access bulletin boards; and an increasing number of organizations, such as supermarkets and banks, offer Internet connection as an 'added-value' service.

SUBSCRIPTION RATES

* Services such as CompuServe and AOL (sometimes called Online Service Providers, or OSPs) combine information, shopping and bulletin-board-like online games with technical help and a GATEWAY to the Internet, for which they charge their clients a monthly subscription and/or an online fee. There's usually a fixed period of Internet access time included in the subscription (say, 30 minutes per day), after which the user pays a fee for each

'thank you for your extra value service'

I'm here to pay
my phone bill

extra unit of time online.
Obviously, this can prove
expensive if you make
regular use of the Net, so
you need to decide whether
the added-value services
compensate for that.

FREE TO BROWSE

✱ At the other end of the
scale there are free-access
ISP accounts for home users
– you pay neither a
subscription fee nor an online
access charge. In fact, you make
no payment other than your phone bill.

watch out for
those big bills

✱ However, when it comes to getting
technical help, a free Internet connection
tends to be EXPENSIVE. Some free-access ISPs
offer no dedicated technical help, others
provide a helpline charged at premium
rates (around 60p or £1 per minute). This
need not be a deterrent, because an
Internet connection is for the most part
trouble-free and, once it is set up
satisfactorily, you shouldn't need too much
technical advice. Nevertheless, be aware!

PAY AS YOU SURF

✱ Pitched somewhere between the OSPs
and the free-access providers there are ISP
accounts for which you pay a subscription,
in return for which you'll receive unlimited
access to the Internet and free or relatively
inexpensive technical help.

WHAT ABOUT PHONE COSTS?

Wherever you travel in
cyberspace, telephone
charges will be based
on local rates. If your
ISP has a lo-call
access number (at
present, 0345 and
0845 in the UK),
you'll pay local call
charges regardless of
whether you're
accessing a Web page
in the next street or on
the other side of the
world. Note that faster
modems move data
around more quickly,
reducing your online
times and hence your
phone bills.

171

do you get the message?

THE MODEM AND THE MESSAGE

* Computers can't communicate directly over the phone. As we saw in Chapter 5, to do so they need a hardware interface called a modem, which translates data into a form suitable for transmission via domestic telephone lines.

modems manage connections between machines

computer shops will help if you ask

HIGH-STREET HELP

All but the smallest villages now have a computer shop with assistants who can set up and install a modem for you for a small fee.

PCMCIA cards are about the size of a credit card

ONLY CONNECT

* An external modem is attached to the computer's SERIAL PORT using a serial cable (also called an RS232 cable).

* Internal modems look and behave like a PC expansion card, such as a sound card or 3-D graphics card. They're installed in the machine in exactly the same way, by locating a free EXPANSION SLOT and plugging the card in.

PCMCIA CARDS

* As well as internal and external modems, there are now PCMCIA cards. *These are roughly the size of a credit card and were developed for use with hand-held computers and other portable machines, but can be used in desktop machines equipped with a PCMCIA slot.*

CHEAP OR CHEERFUL?

* The performance of a modem is governed by the speed at which it can transmit data – its baud rate (see pages 156-59). The fastest modems available for normal telephone lines at the start of the 21st century connect at between 33k and 56K. There are also 28.8K and 14.4K modems. Although these are now regarded as obsolete, they can be acquired at bargain-basement prices and are fine for the financially squeezed.

'I'm financially squeezed'

fast okay we need a performance

faster means smaller bills in the modem world

56KFLEX V. X2

* *As well as the V90 standard, two proprietory protocols* have been devised to achieve baud rates of 56K: namely, 56Kflex from Rockwell and X2 from US Robotics. Most ISPs SUPPORT BOTH protocols. Modems with either technology connect and upload at 33.6K and download at 56K.

TESTING TIME

You can test a PC modem by running the bundled Windows terminal software named HyperTerminal (Start, Programs, Accessories, Communications, HyperTerminal). Launch the program, then type 'test' into the New Connection dialog and click OK. From the Connect Using pop-up list, choose the modem you've installed and click OK. Now type 'AT' and press return ('AT' is the command for 'Attention!' from the ubiquitous Hayes modem command language.). If all is well, the modem will respond 'OK'.

DIAL-UP NETWORKING WITH WINDOWS

* Windows 95 and 98 make Internet connection very easy, and there are only slight variations between the two. You use Windows' Dial-up Networking Wizard to tell the operating system about the connection you want to make, and the rest is handled automatically. Here's how to do it.

use the Windows dial-up networking wizard

STEP 1

* *Double-click My Computer* and double-click Dial-Up Networking. Double-click the MAKE NEW CONNECTION icon. Enter your ISP's name in the Connection Name field and choose your modem from the list (it will probably already be highlighted). Click Next. Type your ISP's telephone number into the appropriate field. Click Next again, and the computer will create a new Dial-Up Networking icon with the name of your service.

type your ISP's name and choose your modem from the list

✱ Now right-click the newly created icon and select Properties. Click the Server Types tab and select PPP from the Type of Dial-Up Server pop-up list. Click TCP/IP in the Allowed Network Protocols part of the dialog. Make sure no other box is checked. Click the TCP/IP settings button and select the relevant IP address options, following the instructions given to you by your ISP. If your ISP has provided primary and secondary DNS numbers, enter them in the appropriate places and check the Default Gateway box. CLICK OK, then OK again.

STEP 2

✱ *Windows is now configured to connect to your ISP*. Double-click the icon that you've just configured for a dial-up connection. Type your user name and password (as chosen by you and approved by your ISP) into the appropriate fields, then click Connect.

✱ The computer will dial the ISP and establish a connection. If all goes well, you'll see the Connected To Provider dialog. This displays a running count of your online time and the speed at which you're connected (which may not be the maximum speed of your modem, if the phone line is noisy or there are other problems). *You can now use Internet applications software*, such as a Web browser and FTP and IRC clients etc.

wait for the wizard
to prompt you

PROMPT REQUEST

When you run Internet Explorer and Outlook Express for the first time, the relevant Wizard will prompt you for some basic information, such as your email address and the address of your ISP's news server.

it's not too hard
if you read the
instructions

GOING ONLINE WITH WINDOWS 3.X

* PCs running Windows 3.x can be connected to the Net - but unlike machines that have the latest Windows version, 3.x does not come with Winsock TCP/IP software. Fortunately, there are plenty of shareware versions available.

it's a blast with Trumpet Winsock

CLARION CALL

* *One of the best shareware TCP/IP utilities is Trumpet Winsock* (you can install and use it on a trial basis for a while free of charge, then if you decide to continue using it you pay a fee).

* Trumpet Winsock is easy to install. It may come to you from your ISP as an all-in-one package, with an automatic installer that decompresses the software and installs it into the correct folders. More usually, Trumpet is shipped as a SELF-EXTRACTING ARCHIVE (SEA) suite of utilities. If that's how you receive your copy, here's how to use it.

TCP/IP UTILITIES

Windows computers use a TCP/IP stack called Winsock that also handles the SLIP or PPP connection to your ISP (see page 85). Windows 95 and 98 machines come with Dial-Up Networking, Microsoft's own TCP/IP stack and PPP utility. Windows 3.x users will require one of the many shareware Winsock utilities, such as Trumpet Winsock or Chameleon Winsock.

Trumpet Winsock is easy to install

TRUMPET VOLUNTARY

✱ Create a DIRECTORY called Trumpet, copy the Trumpet SEA to it and then run it. From the uncompressed files, move WINSOCK.DLL to the Windows System directory. Install TCPMAN.EXE as an icon in the Program Manager group.

✱ Click the TCPMAN icon in the Program Manager group and select SETUP from the File menu. In the Name Server field of the Network Configuration dialog, type the primary DNS number given to you by your ISP; in the Domain Suffix field, type the ISP's domain name.

double speed 1, 2, 3, 4

enter a speed double your modem's rating

✱ Leave the IP address as 0.0.0.0, check the Internal SLIP box, and set the SLIP Port number to the number of the COM port to which you have connected your modem (probably 1, 2 or 3, depending on where your mouse is attached and whether you have an internal modem or an external one). Enter a speed double that of your modem's rating into the Baud Rate field, then CLICK OK.

I go online with
Windows 3.X

CONNECTING WITH TRUMPET WINSOCK

To connect to your ISP, pull down the Dialler menu and select Login. Unless you create a Login Script (Dialler, Edit, Scripts) to automate the procedure, you'll be prompted for the telephone number to dial, plus your user name and password. If all goes well, the machine will dial your ISP and connect to the Internet, at which point you can minimize the TCPMAN window (but don't close it!) and launch your browser or email client, or other Net application. When you've finished, maximize the TCPMAN window, then pull down the Dialler menu and select Bye to terminate the connection.

177

GOING ONLINE WITH AN OLD PC

* Although going online with the latest PC is a lot easier and a much headier experience, there are plenty of truly ancient IBM-lookalikes out there in siliconville, available for just a few pounds and yet still able to provide you with an adequate means to surf.

it's ok to dig out an ancient machine

TREASURE TROVE

With a discarded 8086 PC and 2,400-baud modem (treasures that are junk to those who don't know!) and a copy of Net-Tamer, you can get online, surf the Web, send emails, lurk in the darkest shadows of net news and download files via FTP, all for the most slight of financial outlays.

turn sows' ears into silk purses!

VINTAGE VEHICLES

* *The forerunner of the Pentium-equipped PC was the 486*, a powerful machine able – at the time of writing, at least – to run the latest Windows software.

* Prior to the 486, there was the 386, the fastest PC it was possible to buy around ten years ago. And before the 386, there was the 286 (known as an 'AT' PC); and before the 286, the 8086 or standard XT PC. Believe it or not, even these antiquated computers can be used to get online with free software and a bit of ingenuity.

* It's these two types of PCs, the 286 and 8086, that require special or alternative software to get them connected. All other PCs can use 'standard' WINSOCKS AND CLIENTS.

THE WONDERS OF NET-TAMER

✱ Although there are many possibilities, a truly excellent choice for computers equipped with a lowly CPU is <u>NET-TAMER</u>, an incredible shareware software suite that handles not only all aspects of Net connection, TCP/IP and PPP, but will run a Web browser, email, FTP, Telnet and a Usenet newsreader. Net-Tamer will operate at a VESA screen resolution of 800 × 600 on a 386 machine, or as a text-only program on the lowliest possible DOS-based PC – even one equipped with nothing more than a floppy-disk drive!

✱ The program is shipped as a self-extracting archive and can be found at several sites on the Net (check out the list of Web sites on pages 188-89 for a suitable source).

✱ *Set-up is easy*. Extract the archive and run the READER.EXE program at the DOS prompt. A menu is displayed from which you can customize the program to suit your account details – primary and secondary DNS numbers, user name and password, domain name, POP3 and SMTP mail servers, and so on. It will all be straightforward stuff for those who have absorbed the earlier part of this chapter.

KEY WORDS

CPU:
Central Processing Unit, the electronic 'brain' chip inside a computer (CPU is also often used to mean the main 'box' of a three-box system consisting of a monitor, computer and keyboard)

SELF-EXTRACTING ARCHIVE:
A file created with archive software which runs just like an ordinary program, unpacking its contents in the process

explore the wonders of Net-Tamer

179

GOING ONLINE WITH AN APPLE

✳ The Apple Macintosh requires two pieces of software to establish an Internet connection: a TCP/IP utility and software to dial a PPP link.

'an apple a day would have helped'

Transport systems

Until System 7.5 Apple's own TCP/IP software, MacTCP, was combined with a third-party freeware or shareware PPP client such as FreePPP. With System 7.5 and subsequent system issues, Apple bundled an updated version of MacTCP called Open Transport, together with its own PPP utility called ConfigPPP. Finally, with System 8 (alias OS8) Apple provided a utility that automates the Internet configuration procedure in much the same way as Windows' Dial-Up Network Wizard.

GOING ONLINE WITH OS8

✳ *For those with OS8, the process of going online is therefore a very simple one.*

✳ The first step is to locate the Assistants folder on the hard drive, open it, and double-click the Internet Setup Assistant icon. When the Internet Setup Assistant dialog appears, click Update to create a new ISP account, then click the right arrow to move on to the next stage.

✳ At screen two, click the Add Internet Configuration button and click the right arrow.

✳ At screen three, type an appropriate name for the new account into the field provided (the name of your ISP, for example) and click on the Modem button at the bottom of the dialog. Click the right arrow.

✳ On screen four, choose your modem from the list provided. Select the modem port from the pop-up list below, then click the Tone button (unless your telephone exchange still uses Pulse dialling). Click the right arrow.

✳ When screen five appears, type the ISP telephone number, your user name and password (all of which will be confirmed by your ISP when you get your account).

✳ Click on, to screen six, and check the appropriate button (which will almost invariably be 'No'). Then click the right arrow.

✱ On screen seven, enter the primary and secondary DNS numbers provided by your ISP. Ignore the optional Domain Name field.
✱ Click on, to screen eight, and enter your email address and email password (which will probably be the same as your log-on password).

you need to ask for a modem specifically for the Mac

✱ At screen nine, enter the POP3 and SMTP account names of your ISP's mail service – both of which will probably be the same and look something like mail@sixty3ink.co.uk. Screen ten is where you type the ISP's news server address.
✱ *Finally, at screen eleven, click Go Ahead* to complete the set-up procedure.
✱ If you want the machine to connect to the Internet straight away, check the CONNECT WHEN FINISHED box.

MAC MODEMS

Buy a modem marketed specifically for the Mac. Although the device itself is exactly the same as the (usually cheaper) PC external modem, only the Mac version will come with a Mac serial cable.

PROBLEMS?

If all doesn't go well, re-enter your password – it's easy to make a typing mistake. Also try Pulse instead of Tone dialling. Make sure all the account names and your user name have been typed correctly, too. If all else fails, call the ISP's helpline – especially if your ISP offers free or inexpensive assistance. That's what the service is there for.

'I know, I'll call the help line'

GOING ONLINE WITH AN OLD APPLE

* Apple owners with older versions of the system need to set up their machines for Internet access manually - but that's not as difficult as you might imagine.

sigh

FreePPP
unpacks
itself

STEP 1

* *The first step is to ensure that the computer is equipped with MacTCP* (or the later Open Transport) and a PPP client such as FreePPP (or Apple's own ConfigPPP). All of this software is free and should have come either with your computer or from your ISP when you got an Internet account. If it didn't, contact your ISP.

* Locate the PPP client and click on its installer icon. The example given here uses FreePPP, but ConfigPPP is very similar.

STEP 2

* FreePPP automatically unpacks itself into the correct system extension and control panel folders. It also places an icon in the upper right of your screen on the menu bar. Click the menu bar icon and select Open FreePPP Setup. A dialog will appear, which may or may not be expanded. If it isn't, you need to click on the latch to expand it.

* Click Modem Setup button, and from its dialog select the port to which your modem is connected; click the Tone button, and ensure that the Speaker On and Hangup After Disconnect boxes are

CONNECTING WITH FREEPPP

To initiate and establish a connection with FreePPP, select Open FreePPP Connection from its icon on the menu bar. Alternatively, simply fire up a Web browser, email client or other Internet application, and the FreePPP connection will start automatically. FreePPP reports on the progress of the connection as it initializes the modem, dials the ISP and offers up your user name and password.

checked. Click OK. Back at the General options, check the Allow Applications to Open Connection box.

✻ Now click the Accounts tab and click New. Enter the ISP name and telephone number and your user name and password. Click the Connection tab, and select 115,200bps for the connection speed and RTS/CTS for the flow control.

✻ Now click on the Options tab and enter the primary and secondary DNS numbers provided by your ISP. Ensure that the IP button saying Provided by the PPP Server is checked. Click OK.

✻ Now use the latch to close up the dialog. If it isn't already showing, select the name of the account you've just set up from the Connect To pop-up list. Finally, pull down the File menu and select Quit.

STEP 3

✻ From the Apple menu, select Control Panels. When the Control Panels window appears, double-click the MacTCP icon. Check that the FreePPP icon is highlighted; if it isn't, click on it. Then click the More button.

✻ In the Obtain Address section, click the Server button. Enter the ISP's domain name (e.g. wimpleware.co.uk) in the Domain field, and the primary DNS number in the IP address field at its right. Enter the same domain name below these two, then enter the secondary DNS number. Click OK, then click OK again. Then RESTART THE MAC.

have a nice
apple

Apples use free
internet software

DOUBLING UP

Enter a speed double the speed rating of your modem. Modems use error correction and data compression to squeeze more data into a connection.

click the
server button

always restart the
Mac after configuring

183

IF YOU HAVEN'T GOT A COMPUTER

* If you don't have a computer and there's no hope of buying one, you can still get online in a variety of ways. When public access to the Internet first began to snowball in the mid 1990s, cybercafes began to appear. These otherwise ordinary cafes offered Internet connection, along with coffee, at computers dotted around inside. You go in, pay a smallish fee and get to surf the Net.

one of the perks of being at school is free internet time

Back to school

If you're a student, you'll almost certainly be able to get free access to the Net via a college computer centre, even if your course lacks any computer content. And nowadays even the most underequipped school has at least one connection, though to get at it you may have to fight your way past the tough kids downloading porn or instructions about how to deliver an instantly lethal rabbit punch.

THE TWILIGHT OF THE CYBERCAFE

* Incredibly cheap computers, free ISP accounts and modems all but given away free with boxes of breakfast cereal have rather pulled the plug on the cybercafé, but some are still operating and they are an excellent way of getting online for the terminally short of cash.

hang out at the cybercafe

I don't need email in my line of work

not all
occupations need
the internet

'you should see what
Smithers has been
emailing'

OTHER OPTIONS

*** Many public libraries offer a similar
service**. There's a computer or two in a
corner of the library where, for a small
fee, you can connect up and slip away
into Netopia.

* The employed will almost certainly
find that their <u>EMPLOYERS</u> have Net
connections – though whether as a
street sweeper you can persuade office
staff to let you lay eager fingers on
their jealously guarded keyboards is
another matter entirely. Office
workers shouldn't have too many
problems, though, in bending a
connection to their own purpose.

BIG BROTHER

Be aware that if you
access the Net at work
your employers might
well be monitoring
what you do online
(reviewing the 'history'
lists in your Web
browser is one simple
method). Work is
perhaps not the best
place to subscribe to
erotica or to dash off
multiple emails
offering your services
to competitors in the
same industry.

get online in your
library and liven
the old place
up a bit

APPENDIX
PICK OF THE NET

* The Internet is so rich and so diverse it's unlikely that any two devotees would choose the same favourite sites, but the following list - ranging from the essential and useful to the playful and bizarre - may serve as a handy starter pack for your Bookmarks/Favorites menu.

ABOUT THE NET

* http://www.access.digex.net/~ikind/babel.html
Comprehensive lexicon of Netspeak and Net abbreviations and acronyms.

* http://family.netshepherd.com
Moderated directory of Web sites and Net services with content suitable for families.

* http://www.deja.com
Complete archive of daily Usenet postings with author-profile facilities and free email accounts.

* ftp://rtfm.mit.edu/pub/usenet-by-hierarchy
Usenet FAQs gathered together for convenience by the Massachusetts Institute of Technology.

* http://www.magma.com~leisen/master_list.html
Full listing of Usenet hierarchies.

* http://cs1.presby.edu/~jtbell/usenet/newgroup/
Guidelines for starting your own Usenet group.

* http://www.cis.ohio-state.edu/~barr/alt-creation-guide.html
Ditto for creating alt hierarchy newsgroups.

* http://www.liszt.com
Comprehensive catalogue of mailing lists and IRC channels.

* http://www.coolllist.com
How to start your own mailing list (type that URL carefullllly!).

* http://www.funet.fi/~irc/
Documentation detailing the concept of IRC, together with an annotated listing of available channels.

* http://www.godlike.commuds Awaken your interest in online games.

* http://www.cs.okstate.edu/~jds/mudfaqs.htm
All you need to know to in order to play them.

* http://www.virtual-voice.com Information on Internet telephony.

* http://von.comteleph.html/ More of the same.

* http://ontheair.com Tune in to details of Web-based radio programs.

BOOKS AND BOOKSELLERS

* http://www.amazon.co.uk (and .com)
  The hugely popular online bookshop (UK/US).

* http://www.barnesandnoble.com The Net's biggest bookseller.

* http://bookshop.blackwells.co.uk Academic books of all kinds.

* http://www.waterstones.co.uk The UK high-street book chain's online incarnation.

* http://www.penguin.co.uk (and .com) Penguin online (UK/US).

BUY AND SELL

* http://www.loot.co.uk UK mart for anything and everything.

CULTURE ET AL.

* **http://ipl.sils.umich.edu**
  The Internet Public Library. Books, magazines, academic papers, and more.

* http://classics.mit.edu Indexed archive of Latin and Greek texts.

* http://www.imdb.com The Internet Movie Database.

* http://www.moma.org Museum of Modern Art, New York.

* http://www.nhm.ac.uk Natural History Museum, London.

* http://www.icom.org/vimp/world.html Searchable directory of museums on the Net.

* http://netvet.wustl.edu/e-zoo.htm Online zoo.

EMAIL

* http://rs.internic.net/ Register your Internet domain name here.

* http://www.hotmail.com The Net's leading free email service.

* http://www.whowhere.com
  Find the email addresses of long lost friends and relatives.

MEDIA

* http://www.abc.net.au Australian Broadcasting Corporation.

* http://www.bbc.co.uk BBC.

* http://www.cnn.com CNN (the US news service).

* http://www.guardian.co.uk Guardian.

* http://www.nytimes.com New York Times.

* http://wwwsmh.com.au Sydney Morning Herald.

PRACTICALITIES

* http://www.mapquest.com Detailed maps from around the world.

* http://tycho.usno.navy.mil/ The current time anywhere in the world.

* http://weather.yahoo.com World weather patterns.

* http://www.calculator.com Online calculator for every occasion.

* http://babelfish.altavista.digital.com Instant language translation.

* http://www.thesaurus.com
  Roget's comprehensive lexicon of alternatives goes online.

* http://www.birdseye.com/search.html
  Tempting recipes for frozen foodstuffs.

* http://www.ukonline.co.uk/ukonline/travel/contents.html
  Timetables for anything that moves in the UK.

PROPER PRECAUTIONS

* http://www.condom.com US johnny-come-lately.

SEARCH

* archie.hensa.ac.uk UK-based Archie server.

* archie.internic.net Ditto in the US.

* http://www.altavista.com AltaVista's ETC.

* http://www.yahoo.com
  Great search engine, plus a free email account for those who want it.

* http://webcrawler.com More searching.

* http://www.northernlight.com Ditto.

* http://www.excite.com
  Search engine with a difference. All the sites catalogued have
  been visited and rated by Excite's staff.

SOFTWARE

* http://www.netscape.com Grab a copy of the World's favourite Web browser.

* http://www.microsoft.com Home of Netscape's great Net rival.

* http://www.sun.comjava Home of Java.

* http://www.tucows.com A small planet's worth of shareware for download.

* http://www.shareware.com Ditto.

* http://www.pht.cominfo-mac
  A mountain of Mac software available for free download.

* http://www.adobe.com
  Download a copy of Acrobat Reader and access the
  Net's widely used PDF document file format.

* http://www.eudora.com
  Widely regarded as the best mailer software available,
  both for PCs and for Macs.

* http://www.forteinc.com
  The company behind the excellent Windows net-news client Free Agent
  and its shareware incarnation Agent.

* http://www.netnanny.com
  Porn-and-violence-filtering software for concerned parents.

* http://charlotte.acns.nwu.edu/jln/progs.ssi Anti-virus software for the Mac.

* http://www.thunderbyte.com Ditto for the PC.

* http://www.quicktime.apple.com Animation standard from Apple.

* http://www.real.com
  Download a player to handle streaming audio and video.

* http://www.winzip.com The PC standard for file compression.

* http://www.aladdinsys.com Ditto for the Mac.

* http://deckard.mc.duke.edu/ IRC software for the Mac and PC.

* http://www.pgp.com
  Protect your stuff from prying eyes with Pretty Good Privacy.

* http://www.pgpi.com The international PGP home page.

* http://www.sausage.com Home of the Hot Dog Web editor.

* http://www.columbus.rr.com/ksiders/atari.htm
  Ken Siders' ambitious Net-connectivity software for Atari 8-bit computers.

WACKY/WONDERFUL/WEIRD

* http://www.eeggs.com
  Discover the Easter eggs (games and other surprises) hidden in applications
  software by programmers.

* http://www.shortbus.net/dialect.html
  You could be jive-talking! Translate one dialect into another.

* http://www.babbage.demon.co.uk/morse.html Ditto, but in Morse code.

* http://www.thesmokinggun.com
  Trawl through police records detailing celebrity misdoings.

* http://www.deathclock.com Find out when to pop your clogs.

* http://freeweb.pdq.net/headstrong/
  Wacky science projects for kids, using materials found around the home.

* http://home.earthlink.net/~chellec/ The world's weirdest band names.

* http://www.ask-a-chick.com What girls really think.

* http://www.findagrave.com Dig up your favourite dead celeb.